GIANTS
PAST & PRESENT

DAN FOST

MVP
BOOKS

First published in 2010 by MVP Books, an imprint of MBI Publishing Company and the Quayside Publishing Group, 400 First Avenue North, Suite 300, Minneapolis, MN 55401 USA

This edition published in 2011.

MVP Books are also available at discounts in bulk quantity for industrial or sales-promotional use. For details write to Special Sales Manager at Quayside Publishing Group, 400 First Avenue North, Suite 300, Minneapolis, MN 55401 USA.

To find out more about our books, visit us online at www.mvpbooks.com.

Library of Congress Cataloging-in-Publication Data

Fost, Dan, 1962–
  Giants past & present / Dan Fost.—Rev. ed.
    p. cm.
  Includes index.
  ISBN 978-0-7603-4218-3 (hb w/ jkt)
  1. New York Giants (Baseball team)—History. 2. San Francisco Giants (Baseball team)—History. I. Title.
  GV875.N42F67 2010
  796.357'64097471—dc22

                    2009031133

Printed in China

Edited by Josh Leventhal
Designed by Jennie Tischler

CONTENTS

Photo and Illustration Credits

We wish to acknowledge the following for providing the illustrations included in the book. Every effort has been made to locate the copyright holders for materials used, and we apologize for any oversights. Individual photographers and collections are listed for photographs when known.

AP/Wide World Photos: p. 15 top; 18 top (Sal Veder); 23; 24; 28 top (Jeff Roberson); 33 top (Susan Ragan); 36 (Robert H. Houston); 37 top (Marcio Jose Sanchez); 39 left; 40; 44 (Paul Sakuma); 45 right (Ben Margot); 47 top; 47 bottom (Eric Risberg); 49 bottom (John Rooney); 52 bottom; 53 top (Gene Smith); 53 bottom left (Lenny Ignelzi); 60 bottom (Vandell Cobb/Ebony Collection); 61 left (Robert W. Klein); 62 left and right; 63 bottom (Alan Diaz); 65 top right; 68 left and right (Robert H. Houston); 69 top (Slava J. Veder); 83 bottom (Harry Harris); 88; 93; 120 bottom (Murray Befeler); 125 bottom (Jeff Chiu); 134 left; 134 right (Eric Risberg); 135 left (Eric Risberg); 135 right (Kevork Djansezian) 137 top right (Jeff Robbins); 139 bottom (Kurt Hegre/*The Fresno Bee*); front cover top right (Dan Krauss).

Getty Images: p. 2 (Rob Tringali/Sportschrome); 9 (Michael Heiman); 11 (Jonathan Daniel); 12 right and right (Mark Rucker/Transcendental Graphics); 13 top (Howard Muller/Hulton Archive); 13 bottom (Mark Rucker/Transcendental Graphics); 14 (Bruce Bennett Studios); 15 bottom (Rob Tringali/Sports Chrome); 17 top (Mark Rucker/Transcendental Graphics); 18 bottom (Doug Kanter/AFP); 19 top (Jamie Squire); 19 bottom (Heinz Kluetmeier/*Sports Illustrated*); 22 left (Bruce Bennett Studios); 22 right (Diamond Images); 24 bottom (Ron Kuntz Collection/Diamond Images); 25 (Justin Sullivan); 28 bottom (Jed Jacobsohn); 29 (Chuck Solomon/*Sports Illustrated*); 31 top (Mark Rucker/Transcendental Graphics); 31 bottom (Don Cravens/Time Life Pictures); 32 (John Storey/Time Life Pictures); 33 bottom (Doug Collier/AFP); 35 (Rogers Photo Archive); 37 bottom (Jed Jacobsohn); 38 right (John Medina/WireImage); 39 right (Otto Greule/Allsport); 41 top (Herb Scharfman/Sports Imagery); 41 bottom (David Lilienstein/MLB Photos); 43 bottom (Mark Rucker/Transcendental Graphics); 45 left (Mickey Pfleger/*Sports Illustrated*); 46 (Focus on Sport); 50 top (Eliot J. Schechter); 50 bottom (Jed Jacobsohn); 52 top (Mark Rucker/Transcendental Graphics); 53 bottom right (John G. Mabanglo/AFP); 55 (Justin Sullivan); 57 left (Bruce Bennett Studios); 57 right (John G. Zimmerman/*Sports Illustrated*); 58 left (Bernstein Associates); 58 right (Jeff Haynes/AFP); 59 left (Jed Jacobsohn); 59 right (George Gojkovich); 60 top (Rogers Photo Archive); 61 right (Jeff Haynes/AFP); 63 top (Doug Benc); 65 bottom (Ezra Shaw); 66 (Mark Rucker/Transcendental Graphics); 67 right (Diamond Images); 69 bottom (Ronald Martinez); 70 left (Mark Rucker/Transcendental Graphics); 71 right (Mark Rucker/Transcendental Graphics); 72 right (Brad Mangin/MLB Photos); 73 (Ezra Shaw); 75 bottom (W. Eugene Smith/Time Life Pictures); 76 left and right (Photofile/MLB Photos); 77 top (Mickey Pfleger/*Sports Illustrated*); 77 bottom (Don Smith/MLB Photos); 80 bottom (Otto Greule/Allsport); 81 top (Brad Mangin/*Sports Illustrated*); 81 bottom (Stephen Dunn); 84 top left (Herb Scharfman/*Sports Illustrated*); 84 top right (Brad Mangin/*Sports Illustrated*); 84 bottom (Brian Bahr); 85 (Brad Mangin/MLB Photos); 87 left (Bruce Bennett Studios); 89 left (Mitchell Layton); 89 right (Brad Mangin/MLB Photos); 95 top (Brad Mangin/*Sports Illustrated*); 95 bottom (Ezra Shaw); 96 bottom (Jeff Gross); 97 left (Walter Iooss Jr./*Sports Illustrated*); 97 right (V. J. Lovero/*Sports Illustrated*); 98 right (Mark Rucker/Transcendental Graphics); 99 right (Mark Rucker/Transcendental Graphics); 100 left (Kidwiler Collection/Diamond Images); 100 right (Focus on Sport); 101 left (Diamond Images); 101 right (Mitchell Layton); 102 left (Brad Mangin/MLB Photos); 102 right (Doug Pensinger); 105 left (George Gojkovich); 105 right (Otto Greule/Allsport); 107 left (Michael Zagaris/MLB Photos); 107 right (Brad Mangin/MLB Photos); 108 right (Mark Rucker/Transcendental Graphics); 109 right (Rogers Photo Archive); 110 (Ronald C. Modra/Sports Imagery); 111 top (Jed Jacobsohn); 111 bottom (Al Tielemans/*Sports Illustrated*); 114 right (Rogers Photo Archive); 115 top left (Photo File); 115 top right (Michael Zagaris/MLB Photos); 115 bottom left (George Gojkovich); 115 bottom right (Mitchell Layton); 117 bottom (Nat Farbman/Time Life Pictures); 118 (John G. Zimmerman/*Sports Illustrated*); 119 (San Francisco Giants/MLB Photos); 121 top (Greule Jr); 121 bottom (Jed Jacobsohn); 123 top (Harry Walker/Diamond Images); 123 bottom (Robert Beck/*Sports Illustrated*); 124 top (Mark Rucker/Transcendental Graphics); 124 bottom (Bill Bridges/Time Life Pictures); 125 top (Rich Pilling/MLB Photos); 127 top (Michael Zagaris); 127 bottom (Donald Miralle); 128 top (Nat Farbman/Time Life Pictures); 129 (Michael Zagaris/MLB Photos); 130 (Jed Jacobsohn); 131 top (Jed Jacobsohn); 131 bottom (Justin Sullivan); 133 top (Don Smith/MLB Photos); 133 bottom (Jim McIsaac); 136 top (Rogers Photo Archive); 136 bottom (Mark Rucker/Transcendental Graphics); 137 bottom (Kevork Djansezian); 139 top (Mickey Pfleger/*Sports Illustrated*); front cover bottom (Ron Jenkins/Fort Worth Star-Telegram/MCT/Getty Images); back cover top right (David E. Klutho/*Sports Illustrated*).

Library of Congress, Prints and Photographs Division: p. 8; 10 left and right; 20; 30; 56 left; 74 left; 78 left; 82 left; 90 left; 96 left; 99 left; 116; 120 top.

Library of Congress, Prints and Photographs Division, George Grantham Bain Collection: p. 16; 21; 26; 27 top and bottom; 34; 38 left; 42 right; 43 top; 48; 51; 65 top left; 74 right; 82 right; 86 top; 90 right; 91 right; 103; 104; 108 left; 112 right; 113 top and bottom; 122 left; 126 top and bottom; 132 top; back cover top left.

National Baseball Hall of Fame Library, Cooperstown, N.Y.: p. 42 left; 56 right; 64; 70 right; 75 top; 79 top and bottom; 80 top; 83 top; 86 bottom; 87 right; 92; 96 right; 98 left; 109 left; 112 left; 114 left; 117 top; 122 right; 128 bottom; 132 bottom; front cover top left.

Transcendental Graphics/The Rucker Archive: p. 54; 67 left; 71 left; 72 left; 78 right; 105 right; 137 top left.

Preface and Acknowledgments

Humm Baby! Say Hey! How 'bout those Giants? Like every Giants fan out there, I could not have enjoyed a baseball season more than 2011. As a first-time author, I lived and died with the Giants as they inflicted their special brand of "torture" on the fans. And then I got to join the whole orange-clad, baseball-mad Bay Area in celebrating the Giants' raucous, riotous, long-overdue World Series victory in San Francisco.

So any list of acknowledgments has to start with the 2011 Giants, the famed misfits and castoffs who made watching baseball, and writing about it, so much fun.

And there are others, whose ranks keep growing:

This book would not have existed without the support and encouragement of writerly colleagues Jason Turbow, Frances Dinkelspiel, Al Saracevic, and Danielle Svetcov. (And I'll let Jason Turbow give a nod to the forgotten Giants of his youth, men like Mike Ivie and Fred Breining. I wish I had room for them all.) Bruce Kelley of *San Francisco* magazine gave me the assignment that led to the book and may have reversed the Giants' curse.

Diana Parker, Geralyn Pezanoski, and Alley Pezanoski-Browne of Spoken Media and Susan MacTavish Best and Beth Cook of Best Public Relations brought this book widespread attention.

Josh Leventhal, Maurrie Salenger, James Pfeiffer, and the rest of the amazing team at MVP Books made this book beautiful, and made it sell.

Brian Murphy, Peter King, and the great Gaylord Perry said such kind words for the book's jacket.

As a first-time author, I loved every book event. They are too numerous to recount here, but a few stand out. Thanks to: Dave Kaplan of the Yogi Berra Museum and Learning Center, Bill Kent of the New York Baseball Giants Nostalgia Society, Jay Goldberg of New York's Bergino Baseball Clubhouse, Kathryn Petrocelli of Book Passage in Corte Madera, Rob Fisher of Barnes and Noble, the team at Books Inc., Luann Stauss at Laurel Bookstore in Oakland, David Ulin and the Los Angeles Times Festival of Books, Bob Tobener of the Friends of Marino Pieretti, and the San Francisco Old Time Baseball Society.

Representing all the old Giants believers, I'll single out Bob Leinweaver, who sent my son Harry a 1954 New York Giants cap, which Harry wore for each of the Giants' 2010 World Series wins. It worked! I also have to thank John Mavroudis and Benny Evangelista, whose San Francisco suffering informed and infused this book.

I relied on the works of many great writers, but a few stand out: Henry Schulman and John Shea of the *San Francisco Chronicle*; Andrew Baggarly of the Bay Area News Group; the prolific Nick Peters and his collaborator, Tom Schott; and Frank Graham, Frank Deford, Noel Hynd, and Gabriel Schechter, authors of significant books about the New York Giants. Schechter and Tim Wiles at the National Baseball Hall of Fame in Cooperstown helped with the research as well.

The San Francisco Giants organization has been a first-class partner in this venture, with special shout-outs to former managing general partner Peter Magowan, president Larry Baer, Mario Alioto, Staci Slaughter, Bertha Fajardo, Jim Moorehead (and Jim's predecessor, Blake Rhodes), and Joanne Young of the Giants Dugout store, among many others.

I've been very lucky to have the world's most supportive in-laws in the Barker family: Katie, Louis, Charles, Lulu, Chloe, Oscar, and Neil Barker, Shannon Sullivan, and the amazing Sybil Plumlee, a survivor from the Muggsy McGraw era.

My parents, Marcy and Ken Fost, and my brother Mike Fost, have always encouraged my writing career and nurtured it every step of the way. Thank you so much. You are the best.

The most critical ingredients in writing my first book have been the time, love, and support offered by my two most loyal, patient pals: my wife, Betty Barker, and my son, Harry Barker-Fost. Harry is not only a knowledgeable fan but also a fantastic proofreader and salesman. He both inspired and improved this book. There's no one I enjoy sharing my love of baseball and the Giants with more than you two, and I look forward to many more Giants' victory parades together.

—Dan Fost
San Rafael, California, January 2011

NEW YORK PAST, SAN FRANCISCO PRESENT

One of Major League Baseball's oldest and most successful franchises has one of the richest histories in all of modern organized sport. The Giants ushered in all sorts of innovations, from putting the pitcher's mound 60 feet, 6 inches away from hitters to putting shin guards on catchers, from standing coaches on the baselines to selling Cracker Jack in the stands. With their oldest, most bitter rivals, the Dodgers, the Giants also made baseball a truly national sport, moving from New York to California in 1958.

Giant baseball over the years has produced many of game's most indelible images. The early New York Gothams established professional baseball in Manhattan in 1883 and played at such a level that their manager, Jim Mutrie, declared after a stirring win in 1885: "My big fellows! My Giants!" The name stuck, and within a few years, they lived up to it, bringing home the franchise's first championships, in 1888 and 1889.

In the new century, with baseball ascendant as America's pastime, pugnacious manager John McGraw—"Little Napoleon"—stood alongside tall, college-educated Christy Mathewson and launched an era that netted ten pennants and three World Series winners over the next three decades.

Polo Grounds lithograph, 1887

AT&T Park, 2007 All-Star Game

In the Giants pantheon, McGraw passed the torch to Bill Terry, a disciplined businessman and hitter who, with Carl Hubbell and Mel Ott, helped the Giants to a title in 1933 and two other pennants. Ott succeeded Terry as manager and gave way to Leo "the Lip" Durocher, who presided over two of the greatest moments in team history: Bobby Thomson's "shot heard 'round the world" in 1951, which cemented a stunning comeback and beat the hated Dodgers, and Willie Mays' back-to-the-plate catch in the 1954 World Series, keying an upset victory over the Cleveland Indians.

Mays provided the star power when the Giants moved to San Francisco, but in short order newcomers such as Orlando Cepeda, Willie McCovey, high-kicking Juan Marichal, and Gaylord Perry had the team back in the World Series in 1962 and in contention throughout the 1960s.

Though glory eluded them through much of the 1970s and 1980s, the Giants returned to the World Series in 1989, behind Will Clark and MVP Kevin Mitchell, losing to Bay Area rivals the Oakland A's in a Fall Classic marred by a massive earthquake. Hometown hero Bobby Bonds led the team to the 2002 Series and brought home-run records to San Francisco.

The greatest moment in *San Francisco* Giants history came in 2010, when Bruce Bochy's team of underdogs—after winning 92 games and clinching the division on the season's final day—rallied to the World Series and defeated the Texas Rangers to secure the franchise's first championship since coming to the West Coast 52 years earlier. A million fans turned out for the victory parade.

Through the 2010 season, the Giants have won more baseball games—10,436—than any other team in major league history.

LEAGUES AND TEAMS

Although the Giants have been around longer than most major league teams, they were not present at the formation of the first professional baseball league. That body, the National Association of Professional Base Ball Players, formed in 1871 in a saloon in New York. As that league devolved into a cesspool of drinking, gambling, and players jumping from team to team, a new league—the National League of Professional Baseball Clubs—formed in 1876, with team owners, not players, holding all the power.

In existence to this day, the National League (NL) had eight pioneering franchises, located in Boston, Brooklyn, Chicago, Cincinnati, Hartford, Louisville, Philadelphia, and St. Louis. Yes—even though the league had been formed in New York City, the only New York franchise was based in Brooklyn, which at the time was a separate city. And that team, the Mutuals, was booted out of the league before the second season for refusing to travel to play road games. Other franchises came and went over the years—in Providence, Worcester, Syracuse, Buffalo, Detroit, Cleveland, Indianapolis, and elsewhere—before New York City had an entry in the league.

As baseball grew in popularity, and the people running the league held firm on some basic rules, things stabilized. Against this backdrop, in 1883 a wealthy New York manufacturer named John B. Day picked up the disintegrating team from Troy, New York, moved it to Manhattan, and named it the Gothams.

The Gothams competed on fields where polo was played, and by the end of the 1880s, the team known as the Giants had won two world championships.

Other upstart leagues challenged the National League for supremacy, without success. One notable challenger was the Players League, which was founded in 1890 by Giants stalwart (and lawyer) John Montgomery Ward as a protest over unfair player contracts. The league lasted for one season.

In 1892 the National League absorbed the rival American Association and swelled to 12 teams. After eliminating the teams from Baltimore, Cleveland, Louisville, and Washington, D.C., before the 1900 season, the league assumed the eight-team structure it would carry for the next six decades.

After the small-circuit Western League moved into some of the NL's abandoned cities in 1899, it renamed itself the American League (AL) and in 1901 asserted its place as a major league.

The NL initially fought the AL, and the Giants were right in the thick of it. John McGraw, manager of the AL's Baltimore entry, feuded with league president Ban Johnson. McGraw left

New York Gothams and Boston Beaneaters at the Polo Grounds, Opening Day 1886

New York's George Davis, with other National League representatives, 1895

in 1902 and jumped to the Giants, taking some of Baltimore's biggest stars with him. Although the two leagues had made peace by 1903, McGraw and Giants owner John T. Brush refused to participate in the World Series of 1904. The AL was well established in short order, and the Giants played—and won—the 1905 series.

The leagues retained their structure for many years, with the next major changes coming after World War II, with the advent of commercial air travel. Teams began moving. The St. Louis Browns became the Baltimore Orioles, the Boston Braves moved to Milwaukee, the Philadelphia Athletics went to Kansas City, and then the Giants and Dodgers left New York for the West Coast in 1957 and made baseball truly national.

Expansion came in the 1960s, along with more movement. The creation of a new National League team in New York, the Mets, as well as the addition of the Houston Astros in 1962, was followed by expansion into Montreal and San Diego in 1969. At this point, with 12 teams in each league, Major League Baseball went to divisional formats, establishing league championship series to decide the pennant. The new format came almost too late for the Giants, who had five straight second-place finishes in the 1960s but no postseason play to show for it.

The leagues realigned again in 1994, establishing three divisions and a wild card entry to the playoffs. Naturally, the move was a year late for the Giants, who won 103 games in 1993 only to fall a game short of the division lead.

When interleague play arrived in 1997, the Giants played the first game, against the Texas Rangers. For trivia buffs, San Francisco's Glenallen Hill served as the first regular-season designated hitter for the National League, and Rich Aurilia slugged the first interleague grand slam.

The Giants finally seized the wild card advantage in 2002, squeaking into the playoffs and then rolling to the World Series, only to lose in seven games to the Angels.

San Francisco's Barry Bonds, with other National League representatives at the All-Star Game, 2003

THE GREAT TEAMS AND DYNASTIES

From their first decade, the Giants made it clear that they were a force to be reckoned with in the baseball world. Only six years into their existence, the Giants won back-to-back championships with a squad featuring six future Hall of Famers.

The original Gothams of 1883 formed with such stars as catcher William "Buck" Ewing, slugging first baseman Roger Connor, small but tough pitcher Mickey Welch, and John Montgomery Ward, who played infield and outfield and pitched. Although the Gothams lost more games than they won, these four formed the nucleus of a powerhouse, and when they were joined by pitcher Tim Keefe and outfielder Jim O'Rourke two years later, they were nearly unstoppable.

In 1885 the newly rechristened Giants recorded 85 wins against 27 losses, a .759 winning percentage that still stands as the franchise's best ever. But that team finished in second place, two games behind the Chicago White Stockings, the forerunner of today's Cubs. Three years later, however, the Giants won the title, finishing nine games ahead of Chicago, and went on to beat the American Association's St. Louis Browns in an interleague championship series. The next year, they defeated Cleveland on the last day of the season to squeak past the Boston Braves by a game, then beat the Brooklyn Bridegrooms in the championship series between the leagues.

The Giants' next golden era began with the arrival of ultra-competitive manager John McGraw in 1902, launching a 30-year run in which the team won 10 pennants and 3 world championships. The first pennant came in 1904—when the Giants won a franchise-record 106 games—but McGraw and owner John T. Brush, in their animosity toward the American League, refused to play in what would have been the second World Series. Baseball adopted some new rules, however, and in 1905 the Giants did play in the series—and Christy Mathewson turned in a dominating performance, posting three shutouts in the five-game set.

The Giants under McGraw won three straight pennants, from 1911 to 1913, and added another one in 1917. Although they lost in all four trips to the World Series during the 1910s, McGraw had another dynasty on his hands the following decade. This

1889 World Champion New York Giants

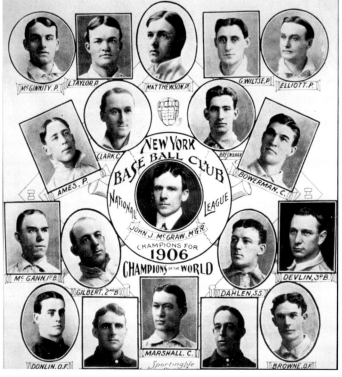

1906 World Champion New York Giants

New York Giants raise the World Champions banner at the Polo Grounds, 1922

time, with a rotating cast of Hall of Famers that included Frankie Frisch, Ross Youngs, George "Highpockets" Kelly, Dave "Beauty" Bancroft, Travis Jackson, Bill Terry, Fred Lindstrom, and Rogers Hornsby, the Giants won four straight pennants starting in 1921. They defeated their ballpark mates, the New York Yankees, in the 1921 and 1922 Fall Classics.

In 1932 McGraw handed the managerial reins over to his biggest star, Terry. Under "Memphis Bill," another Giant dynasty emerged, with southpaw Carl Hubbell on the mound and slugger Mel Ott hitting home runs like no National Leaguer before him. The Giants won the World Series in 1933 and took NL pennants in 1936 and 1937.

1933 World Champion New York Giants

The 1940s were lean years for the Giants, but when owner Horace Stoneham shocked the baseball world by hiring as manager mortal enemy Leo Durocher from the Brooklyn Dodgers, the team responded with two more pennants in the 1950s. Monte Irvin led the hitting and Sal Maglie anchored the pitching in 1951. The win that year was particularly sweet, as the Giants completed a ferocious comeback in the last two months of the season before toppling the Dodgers on Bobby Thomson's famous home run, although they lost the series to the Yankees. In 1954, with Willie Mays in full Hall of Fame form, the Giants beat the Cleveland Indians for what would turn out to be their last championship for decades.

The Giants moved to San Francisco in 1957, and the rebuilt team soon became a consistent winner. They won another pennant—after another playoff against the Dodgers—in 1962 and lost again to the Yanks in a heartbreaking World Series. A team loaded with Hall of Famers in Mays, Willie McCovey, Orlando Cepeda, Juan Marichal, and Gaylord Perry won at least 90 games five more times in the 1960s, but they could muster only second-place finishes for the rest of the decade. Although the team made

only one postseason appearance in the 1960s, it was the only decade in franchise history in which the Giants never posted a losing record in any season.

After a lone division title during the 1970s (1971), another winning era emerged under manager Roger Craig in the late 1980s. Homegrown heroes Will Clark, Robby Thompson, and Matt Williams helped secure the NL West Division in 1987 and the pennant in 1989. In the 1990s, with manager Dusty Baker and the surreal play of Barry Bonds, the Giants were one of the winningest teams in baseball. From 1993 to 2004, only the Yankees and Braves won more games. The Giants won their division in 1997, 2000, and 2003 and reached the World Series as a wild card team in 2002.

Heading into a new decade, fans have hopes for a dynasty in the making. With two-time Cy Young winner Tim Lincecum leading Matt Cain, Jonathan Sanchez, and Madison Bumgarner in a great young pitching rotation, Brian Wilson closing games, and 2010 Rookie of the Year Buster Posey catching them, the Giants were world champs in 2010 and aim to contend for many years to come.

1954 World Champion New York Giants

San Francisco Giants celebrate winning the
National League pennant, October 1962

Brian Wilson hoisting the World Series trophy, November 1, 2010

Giants and Cubs gather with umpires during rematch game, October 8, 1908

FAMOUS PLAYOFFS

The Giants have participated in some of baseball's most celebrated playoffs, on both the winning and losing ends.

The team first tasted heartbreak in 1908, following the infamous game of September 23. On that date, with the Giants locked in a heated pennant race with the Chicago Cubs, 19-year-old Fred Merkle neglected to touch second base as the Giants scored the would-be winning run. Merkle was ruled out on the "bonehead" play, and when the two teams ended the season tied for first, the game was replayed on October 8. The Cubs won 4–2 and took the NL pennant.

Postseason playoffs were extraordinarily rare for many years, as the regular-season winners of each league went immediately to the World Series. In 1951, for only the third time in the twentieth century, two teams ended the season tied atop their league. That year it was the Giants and the Brooklyn Dodgers, as ferocious a rivalry as baseball has ever known. After falling back in the standings by 13½ games on August 11, the Giants rattled off a 16-game winning streak to close the gap. With the Dodgers stumbling to the finish line, the two teams ended in a dead heat after 154 games. The National League called for a three-game playoff to decide the pennant. The Giants took the first game in Brooklyn, 3–1, as Bobby Thomson hit a two-run homer off Ralph Branca (significant, but nearly forgotten nowadays). The Dodgers won Game Two handily, 10–0, on the Giants' home turf, and on October 3 Brooklyn was leading the deciding third game, 4–1, in the ninth inning at the Polo Grounds.

Giants Alvin Dark and Don Mueller led off the bottom of the ninth with singles, and with one out, Whitey Lockman doubled, scoring Dark. Mueller broke his ankle sliding into third and was replaced by Clint Hartung. Dodger manager Charlie Dressen replaced starter Don Newcombe with Branca, who came in to face Thomson. With an 0–1 count, Branca threw a fastball up and in, and Thomson sent a sinking line drive just above the 315-foot

Bobby Thomson is mobbed by teammates following home run against the Dodgers, October 3, 1951

marker in left field for one of the most famous walk-off home runs in baseball history—"the shot heard 'round the world." The Giants won the pennant, stunning the baseball world.

Eleven years later, with the two teams now on the West Coast but no less bitter rivals, the Dodgers once again blew a lead. On the season's final day, Willie Mays homered in the eighth inning to beat the Astros 2–1, and the Dodgers lost to the Cardinals, again forcing a postseason playoff series. Once again, the teams split the first two games, with the Giants winning 8–0 at Candlestick Park but blowing a 5–0 lead and losing 8–7 at Dodger Stadium. On October 3—on the eleventh anniversary of Thomson's blast—the Dodgers took a 4–2 lead into the ninth inning of Game Three. Then the Giants turned four walks and two singles into four runs, with the go-ahead tally coming when Stan Williams walked Jim Davenport with the bases loaded. The Giants held on to win 6–4.

In 1969 baseball adopted its East and West divisions and established playoffs at the end of every season. In 1971 the Giants won the West but lost the best-of-five League Championship Series to the Pittsburgh Pirates, three games to one. The Giants took the first game behind Gaylord Perry's pitching and homers by Willie McCovey and Tito Fuentes, but Pittsburgh's potent offense proved to be too much.

Following the longest postseason drought in franchise history, the Giants won the West Division in 1987 and faced the St. Louis Cardinals in the NL Championship Series (NLCS). The teams split the first two games in St. Louis, and the Giants then took two of three at home, heading back to Busch Stadium with a three-to-two advantage. In Game Six, Cardinal ace John Tudor outpitched Dave Dravecky for a 1–0 win. In the second inning of the seventh game, Giant pitcher Atlee Hammaker gave up four runs, including a three-run blast by light-hitting Jose Oquendo, to end San Francisco's hopes. Jeffrey Leonard, who hit homers in each of the first four games, won the MVP Award for the series, the last time such an award was given to a player on the losing side.

The postseason was kinder to the Giants two years later. Facing the Chicago Cubs in the NLCS, San Francisco's Will Clark set records with a .650 average, 8 runs scored, and 24 total bases. He blasted a grand slam off Greg Maddux in Game One—he later said he could see Maddux tell manager Don Zimmer, "Fastball, in"—but his biggest clutch hit came in Game Five. With the Cubs ahead in the eighth inning and ready to send the series back to Chicago, the Giants loaded the bases against closer Mitch Williams. Clark fell behind in the count and then fouled off two pitches before lining a two-run single that sealed the win.

Jeffrey Leonard homers during Game Three of the NLCS, October 9, 1987

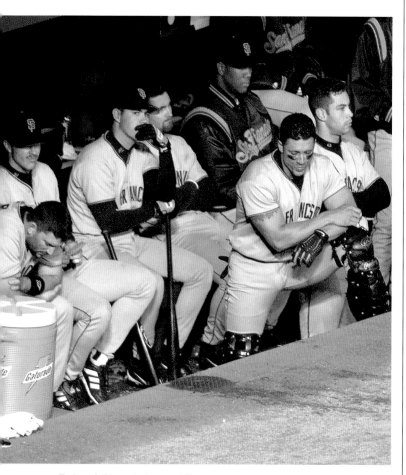

Dejected Giants in dugout following loss to the Mets, October 8, 2000

The Giants faced the Cubs again in a memorable playoff in 1998, when the two teams were deadlocked at season's end in the race for the wild card spot. In a one-game showdown at Wrigley Field, the Cubs took a 5–0 lead into the ninth and held on to win despite a three-run rally by the Giants in the final inning.

In 2000, the Giants' inaugural season at Pac Bell Park, the NL West champs took on the wild card New York Mets, and by all means should have won the series. The Giants won Game One, 5–1, and nearly won Game Two. Down 4–1 in the ninth, J. T. Snow hit a game-tying, three-run home run off Armando Benitez, but then the Mets scored with two outs in the tenth. In the bottom half of the inning, league MVP Barry Bonds (who batted .176 in the series) struck out with a runner on base to end the game. The Mets came from behind to tie Game Three and then won it, 3–2, on a Benny Agbayani solo homer against Aaron Fultz in the bottom of the thirteenth. The Mets closed the series with a 4–0 Game Four victory.

As wild card winners in 2002, the Giants faced the heavily favored Atlanta Braves in the first round. Although the Braves went up two games to one, Bonds brought his bat this time, hitting three homers to help the Giants take the series. After winning Game Four at home, the Giants won Game Five in Atlanta, 3–1, as the Braves stranded 15 runners.

On a roll, the Giants went to St. Louis for the NLCS and won the first two games. Back in San Francisco, they dropped Game Three and fell behind in each of the next two games. In Game Four, Snow doubled in two runs, and Benito Santiago, the eventual series MVP, provided the game winner on a two-run home run. Trailing 1–0 in the eighth inning of Game Five, Bonds drove Kenny Lofton in with a sacrifice fly, and in the ninth, the Giants got successive two-out singles from David Bell, Shawon Dunston, and Lofton to win.

In 2003 the Giants won the division, but in a strange quirk, the wild card Florida Marlins got to play the final three games of the National League Division Series at home, the last time that was allowed. The Giants' Jason Schmidt shut out the Marlins in Game One, 2–0, but Florida took Game Two in San Francisco, 9–5. The Giants came from behind to send Game Three into extra innings and then took a 3–2 lead in the eleventh. But Gold Glove right fielder Jose Cruz Jr. dropped an easy fly ball to lead off the Marlins' eleventh, and a two-out Ivan Rodriguez single plated two unearned runs and gave the series to the Marlins. As in so many other postseason appearances, the Giants tasted heartbreak again.

The torture ended at last in 2010. The Giants won the pennant on the last day of the season and then took on the wild card Braves. Tim Lincecum was at his dominant best in Game One, striking out 14 batters in a 1–0 victory. Luck played a big part in subsequent games, as the Giants rode Braves' errors and injuries to a 3–1 series win. All four games were decided by one run, and the Giants' lone loss in the series came in 11 innings in Game Two.

That put the Giants in the NLCS against the big, bad Philadelphia Phillies. Undaunted, Lincecum outdueled ace Roy Halladay in Game One, and Cody Ross reached him for two home runs. Ross went on to tally six extra-base hits in the series, winning the MVP. Matt Cain threw a shutout, Juan Uribe hit a magical sacrifice fly, the bullpen (led by black-bearded Brian Wilson) was nearly unhittable, and Bruce Bochy managed circles around Charlie Manuel as the Giants completed an improbable upset and headed to the World Series for the fourth time since moving to San Francisco.

David Bell and Rich Aurilia celebrate following series-clinching run in Game Five of the NLCS, October 14, 2002

Cody Ross, 2010 NLCS

Polo Grounds, 1905 World Series

WORLD SERIES

The Giants have a proud World Series tradition, including five championships in New York and some of the greatest moments ever witnessed in the Fall Classic. They've played in 18 World Series, more than all but two other teams: the Yankees and the Dodgers. Finally in 2010, the Giants brought a title to San Francisco, ending years of frustration with one of the most surprising championship journeys ever.

The Giants' championship history began positively. From 1884 to 1890, the winner of the National League faced off against the winner of the American Association in a World's Championship Series. In 1888 and 1889, with some of the most talent-stacked teams of all time, the Giants won the series.

In 1888 the Giants faced the St. Louis Browns in a best-of-11 series. The Giants clinched after eight games, and the teams played two more exhibitions. Right-hander Tim Keefe won four games in the series and allowed only two earned runs in 35 innings. As a team, the Giants stole 38 bases in the 10 games, led by shortstop John Montgomery Ward's 6; Ward also batted .379.

In 1889 a rivalry was born. The Giants defeated Brooklyn, six games to three, the year before the latter team joined the National League. Giants hurlers Tim Keefe and Mickey Welch—having logged 364 and 375 innings, respectively, during the season—were out of gas heading into the series, and Brooklyn won three of the first four games. But pitchers Ed Crane and Hank O'Day took over, and the Giants won five straight to take the title. Ward batted .417, first baseman Roger Connor hit .343 with 12 RBI, and second baseman Danny Richardson hit three home runs.

The formation and growth of the American League after the turn of the century led to the establishment of the modern World Series in 1903. Cy Young's Boston Red Sox of the American League defeated Honus Wagner's Pittsburgh Pirates in the inaugural series. The next year, the Giants won the NL pennant but sat out the series because manager John McGraw and owner John T. Brush refused to recognize the new league's legitimacy.

By 1905, with prodding from Brush, a new set of rules established a series that even McGraw could live with: a best-of-seven format, umpires from both leagues, and revenue sharing. The Giants won another pennant and faced Connie Mack's Philadelphia Athletics in the World Series. Giants star Christy Mathewson turned in the greatest pitching performance ever seen in the Fall Classic: three complete-game shutouts, with 18 strikeouts and 1 walk in 27 innings, all accomplished in a six-day span. Only one Athletics player made it as far as third base against Matty.

Mathewson and McGraw led the Giants to three straight series from 1911 to 1913, but the Giants didn't win any of them. The A's were the victors in 1911 and 1913, while the Red Sox won in 1912.

Although Mathewson was good in 1911, he was not the untouchable force he had been in 1905. He won the opener but lost his next two starts, including an 11-inning, complete-game loss in Game Three. A prolonged rainstorm delayed the series for six days—a precursor to long rain delays in the 1962 series and the 10-day earthquake delay in 1989.

The 1912 series was one of the most dramatic ever, with four games decided by a single run and one game ending in a tie. The Giants ultimately lost on one of the most famous fielding errors of all time. With the series tied at three wins apiece, New York nearly won the decisive game, holding a 2–1 lead in the tenth inning of Game Eight with Mathewson on the hill. Then center fielder Fred Snodgrass dropped a Clyde Engle fly ball for a two-base error. A

Action during Game Four of the 1912 World Series

great catch on the next play did not redeem him; a Tris Speaker single won the series for the Sox.

The A's took their rematch with the Giants four games to one in 1913, as injuries depleted the Giants' lineup. Mathewson threw a 10-inning shutout in Game Two to even the series, but Philadelphia swept the next three, with Hall of Famer Eddie Plank outdueling Hall of Famer Mathewson 3–1 in Game Five.

The Chicago White Sox won the first two games of the 1917 series, and the Giants roared back to win the next two. The tide turned in Game Five, however, when Chicago rallied from a 5–2 deficit to claim an 8–5 victory. The White Sox won Game Six, 4–2, thanks in part to some sloppy Giant defense. Sox star Eddie Collins was caught in a rundown but somehow got between third baseman Heinie Zimmerman, who had the ball, and home plate. Collins outran Zimmerman and scored, sealing the win.

With a new influx of talent, John McGraw had a new dynasty in the making in the 1920s, capturing four straight pennants from 1921 to 1924. In three of those World Series, the Giants faced another emerging dynasty, the New York Yankees. Because the Yankees were the Giants' ballpark tenant, every game of the 1921 series was played at the Polo Grounds. This was also the last year of a three-year experiment in which the series was a best-of-nine contest, as well as the first year the series was broadcast on radio. McGraw, a committed devotee of old-style, scratch-out-runs baseball, hated Babe Ruth, the new star who blasted the unheard-of total of 59 home runs that year. The Yankees won the first two games and then went up three games to two, but after Ruth was hurt in Game Five, the Giants swept three straight to win the series. Yankee ace Waite Hoyt pitched 27 innings and gave up no earned runs, but he lost the clinching eighth game on an unearned run in the first.

Casey Stengel scores on inside-the-park home run in Game One of the 1923 World Series

Program cover, 1933 World Series

The teams met again in 1922, and this time the Yankees could manage only one tie in the best-of-seven set. The Bambino batted a mere .118 while Heinie Groh (.474) and Frankie Frisch (.471) paced the Giants offense. Irish Meusel drove in 7 runs for the Giants, once again besting his brother Bob of the Yanks.

In 1923 Yankee Stadium opened across the Harlem River from the Polo Grounds, and although the Giants' Casey Stengel delivered the first World Series home run in the "House That Ruth Built"—a game-winning, inside-the-park homer in the ninth inning of Game One—Ruth belted three home runs in the series while leading the Yankees to a six-game triumph and that franchise's first title.

The Giants returned to the series in 1924, their fourth straight and McGraw's last. The Washington Senators broke the Yankees' lock on the AL pennant and took on the Giants in one of the most tightly contested World Series of all time. Art Nehf, who had won the seventh games in 1921 and 1922, outdueled Senators legend Walter Johnson in Game One, as the Giants scratched out a 12-inning win with President Calvin Coolidge in attendance. The teams took turns beating each other, never by more than three runs. In Game Seven, Johnson pitched four innings in relief, and the Giants' Hall of Fame infield of Bill Terry, Frankie Frisch, Travis Jackson, and Freddie Lindstrom suffered bad hops and hard luck as the Senators won in 12 innings.

McGraw ultimately turned his team over to his star, Terry, after the 1932 season, and Terry had the Giants playing October baseball again in 1933 in a rematch with the Senators. McGraw watched from the stands as the new Giants royalty—"King" Carl Hubbell and "Prince" Hal Schumacher—shut down the Senators. Hubbell, the league MVP, gave up no earned runs and won two games, and Mel Ott hit .389 with two home runs.

The Giants were back in the series in 1936 and 1937, but they lost to the Yankees both years. The baseball world thrilled at the prospect of Hubbell facing Lou Gehrig and Joe DiMaggio in 1936, and while the Giants ace beat the Yankees in Game One, Gehrig reached him for a homer in Game Four, and the Yanks coasted to a six-game victory. The Yanks were even more dominant the following October. The Bronx Bombers outscored the Giants 23–3 through the first three games. Although Hubbell won Game Four, that was the Giants' lone win, and the Yanks had their second of what would be four straight championships.

The Giants didn't make it back to the World Series for 15 years, but they returned in style. Written off as dead in 1951, they made a stirring comeback from 13½ games out and finally over-took the Dodgers with Bobby Thomson's "Miracle at Coogan's

Bluff." "We had done the one thing we wanted to do," Giant star Monte Irvin later wrote, "and that was to beat the Dodgers. Everything else was a plus." But the team still had a World Series to play, against their old nemeses, the Yankees. The 1951 series featured the October debuts of Willie Mays and Mickey Mantle, as well as the finale for DiMaggio. The Giants won Games One and Three but couldn't hold their lead, and the Yankees won in six.

In 1954 a powerhouse Cleveland Indians team took the AL pennant with a then-record 111 wins. The Giants came into the World Series as heavy underdogs. Another Giants miracle, and some timely pinch hitting, helped key another upset. In Game One at the Polo Grounds, with the score tied 2–2, Cleveland slugger Vic Wertz bashed a 440-foot drive to center field, a home run in nearly any other ballpark. Center fielder Mays turned his back to the plate and ran, snaring the ball over his shoulder in what many believe was the best catch in postseason history. In the tenth inning, pinch hitter Dusty Rhodes hit a 260-foot home run to win the game. Rhodes didn't start any of the games, but he hit .667 with 2 home runs and 7 RBI as the Giants won in a four-game sweep.

It was a thoroughly remade Giants team, now based in San Francisco, that made the next trip to the World Series. The only player from 1954 still with the team was Mays, who had been joined by sluggers Willie McCovey and Orlando Cepeda. Again the foe was the Yankees, and again a tight series whipsawed, with the teams alternating wins. After the Yankees took Game One, McCovey hit a tape-measure home run off Ralph Terry in the second game, and the Giants won with Jack Sanford on the hill. In the Giants' 7–4 win in Game Four, light-hitting second baseman Chuck Hiller delivered a grand-slam home run, the first by a National Leaguer in World Series history. Ultimately, the series all came down to Game Seven at Candlestick Park. The Yankees plated their only run when Tony Kubek hit into a double play in the fifth inning. In the seventh, McCovey tripled off Terry but was stranded. In the bottom of the ninth, Matty Alou reached on a bunt single, and with two outs, Mays smashed a double to right field. The wet grass slowed the ball, and a perfect throw from Roger Maris held Alou at third. Despite McCovey's success against Terry, and with first base open, Yankee manager Ralph Houk let Terry pitch to McCovey. After blasting a long foul, McCovey uncorked a

Dusty Rhodes scores after game-winning homer in Game One of the 1954 World Series

Chuck Hiller belts grand-slam home run in Game Four of the 1962 World Series

rocket line drive—right to second baseman Bobby Richardson. "I still say Richardson was playing me out of position," McCovey said later. "Normally they had a shift toward first, but he was playing me more toward second. Ninety-eight times out of a hundred, I hit a ball like that, and I run for mayor and win." Two months after the series, Charlie Brown exclaimed in a Peanuts comic strip, "Why couldn't McCovey have hit the ball just three feet higher?"

McCovey believed the Giants had so much talent that they would return to the series every year. Instead, the team suffered its longest pennant drought, 27 years. In 1989, under manager Roger Craig, a team led by Will Clark, Matt Williams, Kevin Mitchell, and Robby Thompson brought the Giants back to the World Series. Once there, they faced their neighbors from across San Francisco Bay, the Oakland A's. The Bay Bridge World Series is most memorable for the earthquake that broke the bridge and led to 63 deaths. Still, games were played. The A's won the first two in Oakland. Then, after the quake disrupted play moments before Game Three—at 5:04 p.m. on October 17—the series took a 10-day break for the region to recover from the disaster. The A's

Candlestick Park following the earthquake prior to Game Three of the 1989 World Series

World Series victory parade, November 3, 2010

won the last two at Candlestick to complete the sweep. The Giants never held a lead in the series.

The Giants didn't make it back to the World Series again until 2002. Behind a rejuvenated Barry Bonds—38 years old and having just won the second of four straight MVP awards—the Giants faced the Anaheim Angels, with both teams coming in as wild card entries in the playoffs. Bonds, who had a reputation for not hitting in the clutch, batted .471 with 4 home runs in his only World Series. His homer in his first at bat of Game One helped the Giants win, and his blast against closer Troy Percival in Game Two nearly brought the Giants back, but they lost 11–10. The Angels took Game Three, and then the Giants won a 4–3 squeaker in Game Four and a 16–4 laugher in Game Five. San Francisco carried a 5–0 lead into the seventh inning of Game Six—eight outs away from clinching their first title since 1954. But a historic Angels comeback led to a 6–5 Giants loss. The Angels won the clincher, 4–1, the following day. "The hardest thing," said first baseman J. T. Snow about the Game Six loss, "was coming back into the clubhouse. They had moved the furniture, and there were plastic tarps over the lockers for a champagne party. A party was supposed to happen, and it never did."

The party happened in 2010. Orange fever swept San Francisco, and beard-wearing, panda-hatted fans (honoring Brian Wilson and Pablo Sandoval, respectively) cheered the Giants past the Texas Rangers in five games.

In the first two games at AT&T Park, facing Texas' vaunted offense, the Giants provided all the firepower, scoring 20 runs. Tim Lincecum looked shaky in the opener, spotting the Rangers a 2–0 lead, but the Giants reached Rangers ace Cliff Lee (previously undefeated in the postseason) for seven runs. Freddy Sanchez had 4 hits and 3 RBI, Juan Uribe belted a three-run homer, and the Giants won 11–7. In Game Two, Matt Cain and the bullpen combined on a four-hitter. Edgar Renteria homered and drove in three in the Giants' 9–0 win.

In Texas, the Rangers won Game Three 4–2. In Game Four, on Halloween night, the orange and black bounced back, with rookies Madison Bumgarner and Buster Posey taking command. Bumgarner threw eight shutout innings, Posey homered, and the Giants won, 4–0.

Lincecum and Lee returned to ace form in Game Five. Continuing his "fountain of youth" play, Renteria, the Series MVP, broke the scoreless deadlock with a three-run homer in the seventh. Wilson completed the three-hit, 3–1 victory with a 1-2-3 ninth, whiffing Nelson Cruz to seal the Giants' first championship in 56 years. And bedlam broke out by the Bay.

GAFFES AND CONTROVERSIES

When Giants make errors, they're not just minor miscues. They tend to be, well, giant errors, committed on the biggest stages. Fans discuss and debate them ardently, often for decades.

A century after it happened, Fred Merkle's failure to touch second base in a pivotal game against the Cubs in 1908 remains contentious, but the play is forever known as Merkle's Boner. What is clear: On September 23, the Giants were in a first-place tie with the Cubs. In a game at the Polo Grounds, the teams were tied 1–1 with two outs in the bottom of the ninth. Merkle, a 19-year-old rookie making his first start of the season, singled to right, sending Moose McCormick to third. The next batter, Al Bridwell, singled to center, scoring McCormick.

Fans streamed onto the field, and Merkle, as he had seen so many veterans do, turned and headed straight for the clubhouse—without touching second base. Ensuing events are shrouded in controversy. Cubs shortstop Johnny Evers began calling for the ball. Some say Christy Mathewson ran across the field to bring Merkle back to second base. (Mathewson later testified that he simply ran out to embrace Merkle and admitted that Merkle never did touch second base.) Fans and Giants players may have engaged in a scrum for the ball; some said a fan heaved it into the stands. Evers maintained that he got the ball in time and touched second base before Merkle did; Merkle insisted he made it back to the bag.

Surrounded by angry fans, the umpiring crew did not issue its decision until the next day: The run did not count, and the game ended in a 1–1 tie. National League president Harry Pulliam upheld the umpires' decision (and was so vilified for it that he suffered a nervous breakdown and committed suicide in the offseason). With the teams tied at season's end, the game was replayed, and the Cubs won. Chicago went on to win the World Series that year—their last championship for more than 100 years and counting.

If the Cubs suffered for their victory, Merkle suffered more in defeat. Although he had a respectable 14-year career, his daughter Marianne told broadcaster Keith Olbermann, who has crusaded to clear Merkle's name, "He didn't talk about it much, but he did tell me that as long as he wore a uniform, not a day went by when somebody didn't call him Bonehead, or shout, 'Don't forget to touch second!'"

Fred Merkle

Merkle finally returned to the Polo Grounds in 1950, figuring he'd tolerate the catcalls in order to have a reunion with old friends and teammates. The Giants fans received Merkle warmly, providing him with some measure of peace and closure.

One of Merkle's longtime teammates, Fred Snodgrass, likewise had a distinguished major league career that was marred by a single mistake. In 1912, with the Giants leading the Red Sox 3–2 in the bottom of the tenth inning of the deciding game of the World Series, Clyde Engle lofted an easy fly that center fielder Snodgrass dropped for a two-base error. The next batter, Hall of Famer Harry

Fred Snodgrass

Hooper, roped a shot to deep center, and Snodgrass made a great running catch. After walking the light-hitting Steve Yerkes, Mathewson then faced another Hall of Famer, Tris Speaker. Speaker lofted an easy foul pop that—yes—first baseman Fred Merkle should have caught. But Merkle hesitated, Mathewson called on catcher Chief Meyers to get it, and the ball fell just out of his reach. The Giants should have had three outs and a champagne soaking by now, but instead Speaker called out, "Matty, that play'll cost you the series." And sure enough, Speaker singled in Engle, and a fly ball brought home Yerkes with the winning run. Snodgrass was saddled with having made a "$30,000 Muff," the amount in series winners' shares his error cost the Giants.

McGraw, remembering the great catch, gave Snodgrass a $1,000 raise the next year. Snodgrass hit .275 over a nine-year career and went on to serve as mayor of Oxnard, California. When he died in 1974, the *New York Times* headlined his obituary: "Fred Snodgrass, 86, Dead; Ball Player Muffed 1912 Fly."

Heinie Zimmerman, cheered by Giants fans, 1917

The Giants lost three straight series—becoming the second and last team to do so—and returned in 1917 and lost again. The goat this time was third baseman Heinie Zimmerman. With the Giants down three games to two against the White Sox, Zimmerman overthrew first on an easy grounder by Eddie Collins to lead off the fourth inning of Game Six. Right fielder Dave Robertson then dropped an easy fly hit by Shoeless Joe Jackson. With men on first and third and nobody out, Happy Felsch bounced one to pitcher Rube Benton, who threw to Zimmerman, hoping to hang up Collins off third base. Catcher Bill Rariden moved up the line for the rundown, but when Collins saw no one covering the plate, he broke past Rariden for home. Zimmerman gave chase and nearly caught the speedy Collins, but he was roundly blamed for letting the run score. (A famous explanation, later exposed as the invention of writer Ring Lardner, had Zimmerman saying, "Who was I supposed to throw to, [umpire Bill] Klem?")

Although many people suspected the influence of gamblers in that series, it was never proved. Yet two years later, after the Black Sox scandal roiled baseball, McGraw suspended Zimmerman and Hal Chase on suspicion of throwing games. The two never played again.

One controversy came to haunt the Giants a half century after one of their greatest moments, Bobby Thomson's 1951 "shot heard 'round the world." *Wall Street Journal* reporter Joshua

Candy Maldonado slides for ball during Game Six of the 1987 NLCS, October 13, 1987

Jose Cruz Jr. misses fly ball during Game Two of the 2003 NLDS, October 1, 2003

Prager learned that the Giants, during their miracle comeback that season, installed a telescope and buzzer system in their center field clubhouse, enabling them to steal other teams' signs. Did Thomson know what pitch was coming from Brooklyn's Ralph Branca in the deciding game of the playoff? Thomson couldn't say for sure, while Branca felt the accusation tainted the home run. And Giant and Dodger fans had something new to argue about.

Relocated to San Francisco, the Giants were still susceptible to miscues and controversy. With the Giants leading the St. Louis Cardinals three games to two in the 1987 National League Championship Series, Tony Pena hit what looked like a routine fly ball to right. Giants outfielder Candy Maldonado slid while attempting to make the catch, and the ball rolled for a triple. A sacrifice fly by Jose Oquendo provided the only run that Cardinal ace John Tudor needed, and the Giants lost 1–0. They lost the series the next day.

Sixteen years later, another right fielder muffed an even bigger fly ball. The culprit this time was Gold Glove winner Jose Cruz Jr., who in his only year with the Giants broke Willie Mays' team record for outfield assists in a season (19). In Game Three of the 2003 divisional playoffs against Florida, with the Giants leading in the eleventh inning, Cruz dropped an easy fly ball, igniting a Marlins rally from which the Giants never recovered.

The biggest controversy that dogged the Giants in the new century, however, stemmed from their biggest star, Barry Bonds. Bonds was implicated in the steroid scandals that roiled baseball; he testified before a grand jury in the Balco case, was indicted for perjury in that case, and was named in former senator George Mitchell's report on steroid use in baseball. According to the book *Game of Shadows* by *San Francisco Chronicle* reporters Lance Williams and Mark Fainaru-Wada, Bonds pumped life into his career and won four MVP awards after age 36 by taking performance-enhancing drugs. Bonds has steadfastly maintained his innocence, but after he broke Hank Aaron's career home run record in 2007, the Giants declined to re-sign him. He was indicted in the offseason and has not played professional baseball since.

Philadelphia Phillies fan with sign taunting Barry Bonds, May 2006

Roger Angell once wrote that the Giants hold the "undisputed championship for hard luck—for losing ball games and pennants and championships in bitter, hair-tearing, unimaginable misadventures," and he wrote that in 1958, before the team ever played a game in San Francisco. And San Francisco is where broadcaster and former Giant Duane Kuiper gave the team the mantra, "Giants baseball: torture."

In the earliest years of John McGraw's reign, the Chicago Cubs were the Giants' greatest foils. The poem "Baseball's Sad Lexicon," more commonly referred to as "Tinker to Evers to Chance," about the Hall of Fame double-play combination, was penned by New York sportswriter Franklin Adams. Adams wrote about the "trio of bear Cubs, fleeter than birds. . . ruthlessly pricking our gonfalon bubble, making each Giant hit into a double [play]."

McGraw was a Hall of Fame manager and widely regarded as one of the greatest skippers of all time. It's true that in his 31 years leading the Giants, McGraw won 10 pennants and finished lower than fourth place in the standings only twice in a full season as manager—but McGraw's Giants won only three World Series in that time, losing four Fall Classics during the 1910s.

McGraw's teams were all too familiar with the heartbreak of letting big-game victories slip out of their grasp in the worst ways imaginable. Merkle's Boner. Snodgrass's Muff. The mental lapses and big-stage failures were often laid at McGraw's doorstep.

After the third straight series defeat, in 1913, an article under Christy Mathewson's byline suggested that the players couldn't think straight on the field because they were used to McGraw doing all the thinking for them. The Giants, the article said, are a "team of puppets being manipulated from the bench on a string." This was necessary to win the pennant, Mathewson wrote, but in the World Series, "the Giants blew up. . . . Self-consciousness, overanxiety, and nervousness weighed on our shoulders like the Old Man of the Sea."

The heartbreaks continued after Bill Terry took over for McGraw. In 1934 the St. Louis Cardinals' famed "Gashouse Gang" steamed up from sixth place in midsummer to join the defending-champion Giants in a pennant race. On the season's final weekend, the Cards beat Cincinnati twice, and the Giants needed only one win at home against the woeful Dodgers.

John McGraw, circa 1910

Brooklyn swept the Giants, and the Cardinals won the pennant. "I guess we all made mistakes," Terry said. "Maybe I made more than anybody else."

Longtime beat writer Frank Graham described the 1936 World Series, in which the Giants lost to the Yankees, as "the oft-told tale for the Giants, of disaster following triumph."

Transplanted 3,000 miles to San Francisco in 1958, the team quickly reverted to form. In 1959 the Giants held a two-game lead over the Los Angeles Dodgers with eight games to play, but they managed to lose seven of those eight and finish in third place. The turning point came when Herman Franks joined the team late in the season and offered to steal signs, to give batters an edge. Pitcher Al Worthington, who had become a born-again Christian after a Billy Graham rally in San Francisco, said he'd quit the team if they did it. Shortstop Daryl Spencer said that Worthington's stand had a devastating effect. "You couldn't believe the morale on our team," he said years later. "The bottom fell out."

One of the worst things about how the Giants came oh-so-close in the 1962 World Series wasn't losing Game Seven on Willie McCovey's line drive, although that hurt pretty bad. It was failing

Manager Bill Terry has words with the umpires during Game One of the 1937 World Series

to get back there again. "We weren't really upset," McCovey said about the loss, "because we thought we were going to be there the next 10 years. We thought we had that good of a team, and that much youth. We thought, 'This is a bump in the road.'"

Instead, from 1965 to 1969, the Giants tallied five consecutive second-place finishes. (In 1963 they finished third, and in 1964 they finished fourth, but only three games back.) In 1965 the Giants lost the pennant by a mere two games to the Dodgers. San Francisco blew a 4½-game lead in September when the Dodgers won 13 straight. The Giants came even closer in 1966, challenging to the final week before falling 1½ games short, again to Los Angeles.

After years of futility, the Giants finally found themselves in another pennant race in 1982. Despite a stirring comeback against the Astros on September 30, keyed by journeyman Ron Pruitt's "Super Blooper," the Giants proceeded to lose two at home to the

San Francisco Giants starting lineup, 1959

Dave Dravecky, August 1989

Dodgers and were eliminated. But sadness mixed with schadenfreude when a Giants win the next night knocked L.A. out of the playoffs.

One of the saddest moments for Giants fans came with the saga of Dave Dravecky, a beloved pitcher in the 1980s. He helped the team win the division in 1987, but in 1988 doctors found a cancerous tumor in his arm. In August 1989, he completed an improbable comeback and won his first start with the team. But in his second start, he began to pitch poorly in the sixth inning. Then, with a loud crack, his humerus bone snapped. "It sounded like a rifle shot," said Duffy Jennings, the Giants publicist at the time. "I'm three decks up, and I could hear him shout." On the ambulance ride to the hospital, when Jennings figured Dravecky would be pondering the end of his career, the pitcher stunned the PR man: "He says, 'What's going on in the game?' They won, and he was 2–0 that year. It blew me away."

As it happened, the Giants won the pennant that year. In the victory celebration, Dravecky broke his arm again, and doctors confirmed the worst: cancer had returned. His baseball career was over. Dravecky's left arm was amputated in 1991, and he launched a career as a motivational speaker.

The earthquake of 1989 brought its own drama and disappointment and put baseball in perspective as the Bay Area dug out from the disaster. Within a few years, the Giants were sold and nearly moved to Florida, until a local group intervened and kept the team in San Francisco.

In 1993 the team's new owners brought in Dusty Baker as manager and signed Barry Bonds as a free agent. The team rolled to 103 wins. Locked in a race with the Braves for the division title, owner Peter Magowan brought his two "good luck charms"—Bobby Thomson and Willie Mays—to Los Angeles for the final four games of the season. "We won Thursday, we won Friday, and we won Saturday," Magowan recalled. "We've got to win a fourth time. The Braves won. My good luck charms ran out."

In that final game, on October 3—the anniversary of Thomson's home run, as well as other stirring Giant wins—rookie Salomon Torres gave up 5 hits, 5 walks, and 3 runs in $3\frac{1}{3}$ innings, and the Giants were shelled 12–1. Despite posting the most regular-season victories since 1962, the Giants finished the year in second place. Naturally, there was no wild card; that came the next year, along with the Braves' move to the NL East.

The loss was, in a way, a precursor to other heartbreaks that followed in what has become known as the Bonds era. There were tough losses in 1997, 1998, 2000, and 2003 (recounted in the "Famous Playoffs" chapter), as well as two others that stand out.

Dejected Giants players in the dugout, September 1993

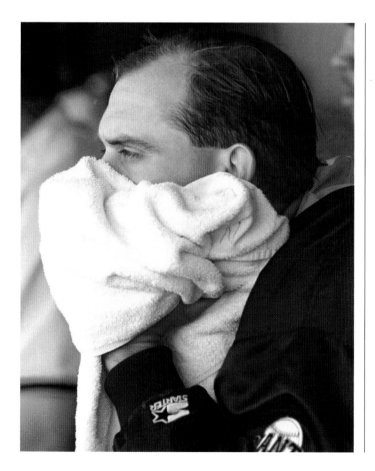

In 1998 the Giants had a chance to clinch the wild card and avoid facing the Cubs in a one-game playoff. All they had to do was beat the lowly Colorado Rockies on the last day of the season. But the Giants' 7–0 lead in the fifth inning was not safe, and the game entered the bottom of the ninth with the score tied 8–8. The Giants' fireballing relief ace Robb Nen faced light-hitting Neifi Perez in an apparent mismatch, but—great Jose Oquendo's ghost!—Perez homered to deep right to force the Giants into a do-or-die playoff against the Cubs.

In 2001 Bonds had one of baseball's magical seasons. In a game against the Dodgers at AT&T Park, he broke the single-season home run record, hitting numbers 71 and 72 off Chan Ho Park. (He finished with 73.) But the Dodgers won the slugfest, 11–10, eliminating the Giants from the playoff race.

The Giants finally turned heartbreak on its ear in 2010. Following Kuiper's lead, fans wore "Torture" T-shirts, and players adopted the mantra, as it referred not only to losing but also to narrow, gut-wrenching wins. Owning their tortured past, the Giants finally shed it and took home the trophy.

Kirk Rueter, during loss to Colorado in last game of the season, September 27, 1998

Giants manager John McGraw (left) and Dodgers manager Wilbert Robinson, 1915

THE GIANTS–DODGERS RIVALRY

No two teams in professional sports have had a longer or bitterer rivalry than the Giants and the Dodgers. Their feud has stood the test of time and geography, moving from a contest between teams in the same city to one between teams in competing cities of the same state.

The rivalry was born in 1889, when a precursor to the Dodgers, the Brooklyn Bridegrooms, won the American Association title and played the NL-champion Giants in the World's Championship Series. The Giants won, six games to three, and the next year Brooklyn joined the National League. In an 1890 game, a Brooklyn coach pretended to be a base runner, drawing a throw and igniting a fight with the Giants.

Brooklyn took on many names in the early twentieth century (Grooms, Superbas, Robins) but rarely put up much of a challenge to the Giants, who were one of baseball's dominant teams. Still, the team from Brooklyn had its moments. The Giants represented Manhattan—"the darlings of the brownstone set," according to writer Frank Graham. Brooklyn became a borough of New York in 1898, but the Dodgers—"dem Bums"—maintained the working-class identity.

Giants manager John McGraw had been a friend and teammate of Wilbert Robinson on the old Baltimore Orioles,

and McGraw hired "Uncle Robbie" as a coach. In 1913 McGraw initiated a feud with Dodgers owner Charles Ebbets. Then he and Robinson suffered a break that led to Ebbets hiring Robinson as manager. McGraw brought all his players into the feud with Brooklyn, and by adding Robinson to the mix, Frank Graham wrote, "it gave new zest to the hate he had thrown on Brooklyn just when it seemed about to wane because the Dodgers were chronic dwellers in the second division."

The Dodgers were still laggards when Bill Terry, Hall of Fame first baseman and manager of the Giants, famously asked before the 1934 season, "Is Brooklyn still in the league?" The Dodgers got revenge by beating the Giants in the last two games of the season, allowing the St. Louis Cardinals to take the pennant.

In 1937 pitcher Freddie Fitzsimmons summed up the rivalry after learning that he had been traded from the Giants to the Dodgers: "It was the blackest day of my life. . . . What was I going to Brooklyn for? I was a Giant, and for years I had hated the Dodgers, and it almost made me sick to think that I had been traded to them."

The fans took the rivalry pretty seriously too. In July 1938, after a Giants victory, some Giants fans began taunting a Dodgers fan in a bar in Brooklyn. The Dodgers fan, Robert Joyce, left the bar, returned with a gun, and killed Giants fan Frank Krug.

Starting in the 1940s under Branch Rickey, the Dodgers found their groove and became a league powerhouse, winning three pennants in the decade. Then Giants owner Horace Stoneham mortified the fans by hiring Leo Durocher from the hated Dodgers as manager. (Durocher was a veteran of many fabled battles in the larger war, such as his brawl with Giants first baseman Zeke Bonura in 1939.) Durocher dismantled the slugging Giants of Mel Ott and Johnny Mize and built a scrappy team in his own image, with such players as Eddie Stanky and Alvin Dark.

The turnabout was complete by 1951, when legend has it that Brooklyn manager Charlie Dressen supplied his own Bill Terry moment with the declaration, "The Giants is dead." To the contrary, the Giants rallied from 13½ games back to tie the Bums at season's end. Bobby Thomson delivered the coup de grace with history's most famous home run to hand the pennant to the Giants.

The story goes that when Jackie Robinson was traded to the Giants after the 1956 season, he retired rather than play for his archenemies. A letter in the files of baseball's Hall of Fame indicates otherwise, however. In it, Robinson assures Stoneham, "My retirement has nothing to do with my trade to your organization." He even wished Stoneham "continued success."

In 1958 the rivalry moved to California, and the Giants defeated the Dodgers in the first game played on the West Coast. It was odd for the two teams to conspire on the move, but the teams sought to retain their rivalry by taking advantage of a natural northern–southern rivalry within California. It wasn't long before they began battling in pennant races.

While the Dodgers edged the Giants out in 1959, the Giants staged a small-scale re-enactment of 1951 three years later. The black and orange came back from four games out to tie L.A. on the last day of the season and then came back in the ninth inning of the playoff finale to win the pennant.

Giants and Dodgers scuffle at Ebbets Field, April 1953

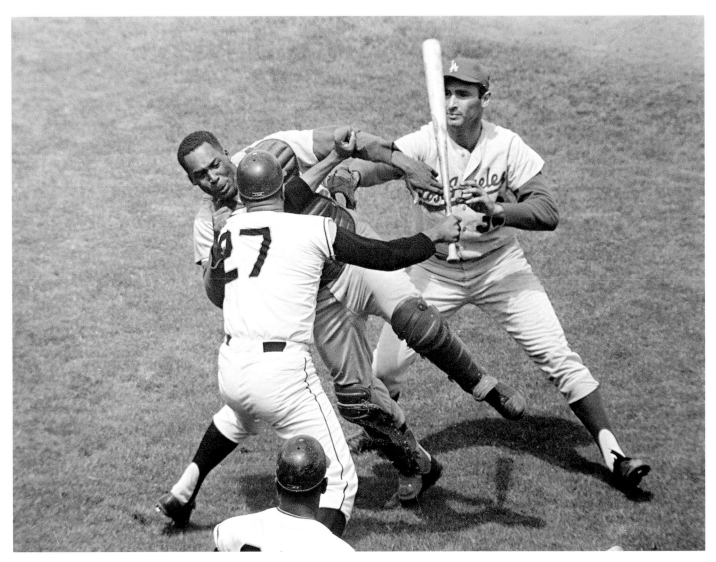

Juan Marichal attacks John Roseboro with his bat, August 1965

The Dodgers ruled the 1960s behind aces Sandy Koufax and Don Drysdale. Things got particularly heated in a 1965 game after Juan Marichal threw some brushback pitches to Dodger hitters. Koufax refused to retaliate, so catcher John Roseboro buzzed Marichal on a throw back to the mound, and Marichal shocked everyone by cold-cocking Roseboro with his bat. Roseboro needed 14 stitches, Marichal was suspended for eight games, and although the Giants won the game (thanks to a Mays homer), the Dodgers won the pennant.

The Dodgers squeaked past the Giants in 1966 as well, and the Giants finally won in 1971, staving off a late-season L.A. charge.

In 1978 the Dodgers' Reggie Smith charged into the stands at Candlestick Park to take on a fan who was throwing things at him. Smith did it again in 1981, but a year later he signed with the Giants as a free agent.

Since then, each team has developed the knack of joyfully knocking the other out of the playoffs.

In 1982 the Dodgers, Giants, and Braves were locked in a three-way race, and the season came down to a Dodgers–Giants series in San Francisco. Two Dodger wins eliminated the Giants, who then exacted revenge when a Joe Morgan home run off Terry Forster—on October 3, Bobby Thomson day—knocked out the Dodgers.

The Giants beat the Dodgers in two out of three on the final weekend of 1991 to keep the men in blue out of the playoffs, and the Dodgers dashed the Giants' hopes in 1993, winning the season's finale 12–1 to allow Atlanta to clinch the division.

In September 1997, the Giants were one game back entering a two-game series at Candlestick. Barry Bonds blasted a two-run home run in the first inning and twirled around home plate after he hit it, stunning the Dodgers. "It was crushing," said L.A.'s Eric Karros. The Giants won 2–1. Bonds homered again the next day, but the really big blow came in the twelfth inning, when backup catcher Brian Johnson won it with a walk-off homer.

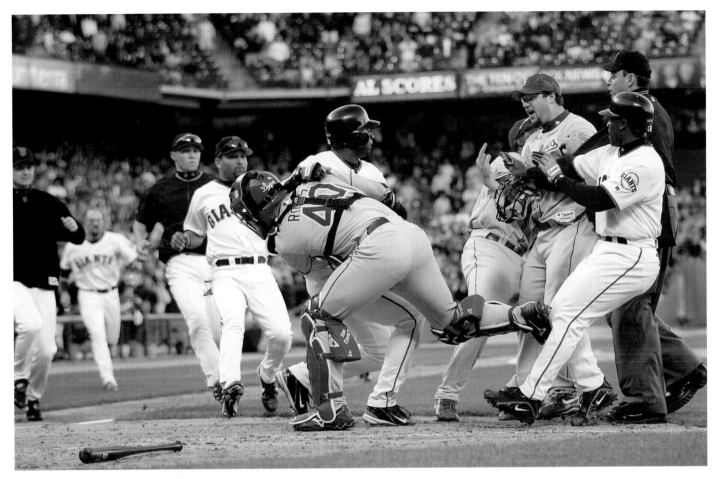

Giants and Dodgers scuffle, June 2004

The Giants won the West by two games.

While the Giants consistently fielded stronger teams in the 1990s, the Dodgers managed to serve as dream wreckers. In 2001 Bonds set the single-season home run record in a game against the Dodgers, but L.A. won and eliminated the Giants in the same game.

In 2004, with both teams vying for a playoff spot, the Giants took a 3–0 lead into the ninth inning on the season's penultimate day. Then came one of those epic collapses: two singles, three walks, and an error had the game tied and the bases loaded. Then Dodger Steve Finley blasted a grand slam to win the game and the division. Even though the Giants won 10–0 the next day, Houston nudged San Francisco out of the wild card.

In recent years, no one gets booed at AT&T Park like a former Giant wearing Dodger blue. Just ask Jeff Kent or Jason Schmidt. Juan Uribe, a 2010 World Series hero for the Giants, broke many hearts in San Francisco when he signed with the Dodgers in the offseason.

Since 1901 the two teams have played more head-to-head games than any other rivals in baseball. As of the end of 2010, the Giants have won 1,099 games to the Dodgers' 1,084.

Dodgers second baseman Jeff Kent hears it from Giants fans, June 2005

CROSSTOWN AND CROSS-LEAGUE RIVALS:
THE YANKEES AND A'S

John McGraw (right), with Babe Ruth, exhibition game,
October 1923

Barry Bonds (right), with Yankee Derek Jeter, interleague play,
June 2007

Think Giants' rivalry and you immediately think of the Dodgers. No other team can equal that special level of hatred. But oddly enough, while the Giants have battled foes from the Cubs to the Braves to the Cardinals in thousands of games over the years, the team's two biggest, longest-standing rivals come from the American League: the Yankees and the A's.

The Yankees, and the Highlanders that preceded them, were not much threat to anyone during the first two decades of the twentieth century. The Giants even rented their home, the Polo Grounds, to the Yankees starting in 1912. But when the pinstriped crew obtained Babe Ruth in 1919, reversing their fortunes forever, McGraw could not abide what he regarded as the long-ball freak show, and he ordered them evicted.

Before they could get their new Yankee Stadium built, just across the Harlem River from the Polo Grounds, the Yanks managed to win two pennants and faced the Giants in both World Series. The Giants prevailed in 1921 and 1922, but in the rematch

John McGraw, with A's manager Connie Mack, 1911 World Series

in 1923, with "the House That Ruth Built" open for business, the Yankees won their first-ever title. Just prior to the series, the two teams played an exhibition game to raise money for former owner John B. Day. Ruth played for the Giants, donning an ill-fitting uniform and homering over the Polo Grounds' right field roof.

Ruth and the Yankees were just getting started. The franchise's glorious dynasty run included World Series defeats of the Giants in 1936, 1937, 1951, and 1962.

Since interleague play started up in 1997, the occasional Yankees–Giants games have always drawn interest. High points included a Barry Bonds versus Roger Clemens matchup at Yankee Stadium in 2002. Clemens vowed before the series to hit Bonds on his elbow guard and then made good on the threat; he also walked Bonds three times, draining the confrontation of its drama. In 2007 the Yankees visited San Francisco for the first time since the 1962 series, and the Giants won two out of three.

In the early part of the last century, the A's had a dynasty of their own in Philadelphia, and the Giants were their principal World Series foe. The Giants faced them in 1905, shutting them down behind Christy Mathewson, and then lost in 1911 and 1913. John McGraw derisively called the A's a white elephant, only to have the team adopt the animal as its mascot.

The A's preceded the Giants in moving west, forsaking Philadelphia for Kansas City in 1955. While the Giants established Major League Baseball in the Bay Area in 1958, they were joined 10 years later when the A's arrived in Oakland from Kansas City.

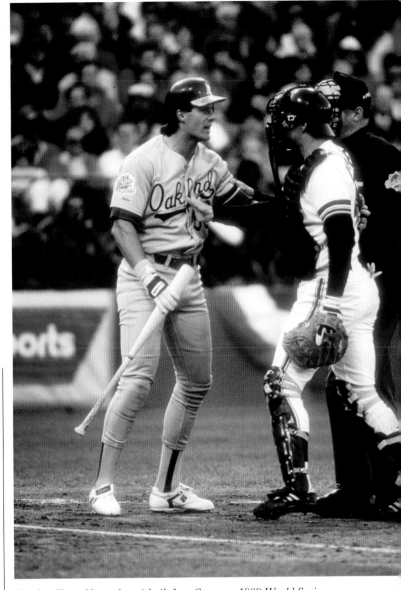

Catcher Terry Kennedy, with A's Jose Canseco, 1989 World Series

San Francisco and Oakland usually play a preseason exhibition, and the two teams take friendly jibes at each other in offseason baseball luncheons. Things got serious in 1989, however, when they both made it to the World Series. The matchup was declared "Baseball Heaven" in the local press, and it even engendered hats with both teams' logos. The excitement turned sour when a major earthquake struck, rupturing the very Bay Bridge that had given the series its nickname. The A's won a long-delayed four-game sweep.

Annual matchups in interleague play help keep the rivalry sharp, particularly as both squads found themselves in contention in the 2000s. The teams split their head-to-head series in each of the first four years of interleague play; through 2010 the A's have a 42–38 overall advantage.

Manager John McGraw (second row, center), with National League All-Stars, July 1933

ALL-STAR GAMES

The Giants have left their mark on baseball's Mid-season Classic ever since the first one, in 1933, when John McGraw came out of retirement to manage the National League squad. The American League won behind a Babe Ruth home run, but the most memorable moment in All-Star history came the next year, when the Giants played host at the Polo Grounds.

In that contest, Giants lefty Carl Hubbell struck out five future Hall of Famers in a row: Ruth, Lou Gehrig, Jimmie Foxx, Al Simmons, and Joe Cronin. After Hubbell came out after three innings, the AL racked up nine runs and won the game.

The game again was played at the Polo Grounds in 1942, moved from Ebbets Field because it held more people, and proceeds were donated to benefit the war effort. Giants sluggers Mel Ott and John Mize went a combined 0 for 6, and Hubbell and Cliff Melton made the squad but did not pitch.

It wasn't until the Say Hey Kid landed on the scene that the Giants really made a mark on the annual All-Star Game. In the words of Ted Williams, "They invented the All-Star Game for Willie Mays."

Indeed, Mays played in 22 All-Star Games as a Giant (and two as a Met) and set many All-Star records, including most at bats (75), runs (20), and hits (23). He shares the record for triples, extra-base hits, and total bases.

Mays homered to lead off the 1965 All-Star Game, delivered a pinch-hit home run off Whitey Ford in 1956, and brought home two All-Star MVP awards (1963 and 1968), although they didn't start handing out the award until 1962, when Mays had already played in 11 games. During the 1961 contest in San Francisco, he doubled in the tying run in the tenth inning and then scored the winning run on Roberto Clemente's single.

That first All-Star Game in San Francisco is remembered for another reason, however. A gust of wind led Giants pitcher Stu

Miller to sway and get called for a balk, forever cementing the reputation of Candlestick Park.

Mays was never alone at the game. Juan Marichal was an all-star every year from 1962 to 1969 and again in 1971. He pitched in eight games and posted a 0.50 ERA, including 14 straight shutout innings, and was named the 1965 All-Star MVP. Willie McCovey, a six-time all-star, took MVP honors in 1969 thanks to a pair of monster blasts off Blue Moon Odom and Denny McClain.

The game returned to Candlestick in 1984, the fiftieth anniversary of Hubbell's feat. The NL's Fernando Valenzuela struck out the side in the fourth, and Dwight Gooden—at 19 the youngest player in All-Star history—did the same in the fifth.

For the 2007 contest at AT&T Park, Mays was honored before the game and threw out the ceremonial first pitch in front of a sellout crowd. Barry Bonds, winner of the 1996 home run derby, disappointed fans when he refused to participate in the contest in the park where he had clobbered so many "splash hits."

In the 2010 All-Star Game, Brian Wilson tossed a scoreless inning to help the NL win—and secure home field advantage for the Giants in the World Series, as it turned out.

Willie Mays scoring after home run, 1960 All-Star Game

Pre-game ceremony at AT&T Park, 2007 All-Star Game

THE OWNERS

John B. Day

Jim Mutrie (right), with John McGraw, 1930s

John B. Day, a wealthy young tobacco merchant, fancied himself a baseball player. But after a disastrous outing on the mound in an amateur game in Brooklyn in about 1879, he found himself in the stands sitting by another man in his twenties. The man, Jim Mutrie, offered to help Day put together a first-rate ball club. Day burned with the ambition to do so, and the two men formed a partnership that made baseball history.

Day and Mutrie formed the New York Metropolitans, or Mets, in 1880, installing them on a polo field in Manhattan. By 1883 the two men established a new team in the fledgling National League, the Gothams, with stars from the disbanded Troy franchise. Day owned the team through its championship years of 1888 and 1889, but he hit financial trouble when his star, John Montgomery Ward, started the new Players League and brought many of the best Giants with him.

After taking on debt and siphoning his tobacco money to the team, Day finally had to sell. New York lawyer Edward Talcott took ownership, but another lawyer, Andrew Freedman, started secretly buying up shares in the name of circus impresario James A. Bailey. By 1895 Freedman owned the team, launching the most tumultuous era in Giants history.

History books are not kind to Freedman. One notes his "breathtaking arrogance, appalling miserliness, and uncompromising dishonesty," saying that his stewardship of the Giants was "a textbook example of how a profitable business could be run into the ground." Freedman, a close associate of New York's unscrupulous Tammany Hall political machine, is sometimes called the George Steinbrenner of his day, as he went through 12 managers in seven years—two of them twice. Former owner John B. Day even served a stint as manager.

Freedman fought with players and the press, sometimes physically. Hall of Famer Amos Rusie sat out a year. One of Freedman's managers was a circus actor. Another tried to move Christy Mathewson to first base.

In Freedman's last act as owner, he saw an opportunity to needle a foe, the old Baltimore Orioles, and hired their manager,

John T. Brush (left), 1910

Charles Stoneham (left), with John McGraw, 1930s

John McGraw. He then sold the team to John T. Brush. The two moves ushered in the Giants' greatest era.

Brush, an Indianapolis clothing manufacturer, gave McGraw free rein to run the team, and he built a winner. When the old wooden Polo Grounds burned in 1911, Brush moved quickly to erect a concrete-and-steel stadium, which stood until 1964. For a time, it was named for him.

Brush died at age 67, a month after the Giants lost the 1912 World Series. His daughters took over ownership, with son-in-law Harry Hempstead overseeing the team. Hempstead usurped some of McGraw's control, but in 1919 he sold the team to a group led by Wall Street operator Charles A. Stoneham. One story has it that Stoneham's son, Horace, penned an essay on what he would do with one million dollars. He wrote, "I'd buy the Giants"; the father then bought the team to help realize his son's dream.

With Stoneham's acquisition, McGraw was able to purchase minority interest and regain baseball control, which led to four pennants and two championships. Stoneham, however, had many unsavory business dealings, including a Havana racetrack, and questionable investment operations that were often the subject of lawsuits. Under pressure from Commissioner Kenesaw Mountain Landis, Stoneham sold it all but kept the Giants.

He died in 1936, passing the team to Horace, then age 32. Horace Stoneham owned the Giants longer than anyone, and ultimately he made the biggest move, taking the team from New York to San Francisco. The old crumbling Polo Grounds lacked parking for a new suburban audience, and attendance was

Bob Lurie, with San Jose mayor Susan Hammer, January 1991

dwindling. "I feel sorry for the kids," he said, "but I haven't seen many of their fathers recently."

Stoneham was also the rare owner who had no business interest outside baseball. The shy owner was known for watching games from his office above the Polo Grounds' center field clubhouse. He also liked his liquor; fellow owner Bill Veeck once wrote, "Horace Stoneham has two occupations in life. He owns the San Francisco Giants and he drinks." But he remained what Roger Angell called "a pure baseball man, a model owner."

By the 1970s, with the team in a funk and Candlestick Park a laughingstock, Stoneham was ready to sell. Buyers were ready to move the Giants to Toronto. And in stepped a local hero, Bob Lurie, a real estate magnate who had been a board member of the Giants since 1958. Lurie helped reverse the team's fortunes on the field, ultimately presiding over the first trip back to the World Series since 1962, but he also had the difficult challenge of trying to replace Candlestick. He characterized his years in the owner's box as "a fabulous, wonderful, frustrating, disappointing, exciting experience."

In 1991 Lurie came to an agreement with the nearby city of San Jose to relocate the team, which ultimately fell through. Exasperated, he went the same route as Stoneham, looking for a buyer. When a group from St. Petersburg, Florida, agreed to buy the team after the 1992 season, the city of San Francisco again went up in arms. A group of local businesspeople, led by Peter Magowan, a scion of Merrill Lynch and former CEO of Safeway, came to the rescue.

Magowan had grown up a Giants fan in New York, baptized in the Bobby Thomson home run. When the Giants left New York, he was heartbroken. "How do you explain that to a 14-year-old?" he said years later. Magowan immediately signed Barry Bonds—before he had even closed the deal to buy the team—and hired Dusty Baker as manager, ushering in an era of success. He led the construction of a gorgeous, privately financed downtown ballpark and a team that went to another World Series. "It was okay to lose the 1951 World Series," he said, because the Thomson homer beat the Dodgers. "It was not okay to lose the 2002 World Series."

Peter Magowan, December 1992

Bill Neukom, October 2008

Magowan and general manager Brian Sabean came under fire in baseball's Mitchell Report for not putting a stop to reported steroid dealing in the Giants clubhouse, particularly by Bonds' personal trainer Greg Anderson.

While Magowan served as the team's managing general partner, the largest shareholder was Harmon Burns, vice chairman of the global financial investment management firm Franklin Resources. When Burns died in 2006, that role passed to his wife, Sue, who died in 2009. The Burns were well liked by players, but they avoided attention and were not well known to most Giants fans.

Magowan stepped aside after the 2008 season, and another member of the ownership group, Bill Neukom, took over as managing general partner and CEO. The ownership roster lists 30 people and other entities, including Giants broadcasters KNBR radio and KTVU television.

Neukom, a Bay Area native, grew up next door to the general manager of the old San Francisco Seals, and his father had given him 10 shares in the Giants when they arrived from New York. A white-haired, bow-tied former chief lawyer for Microsoft, Neukom joyously celebrated when the team delivered a title in only his second year at the helm.

Chub Feeney (left), with Stan Musial and Willie Mays, 1960s

General managers are a relatively recent phenomenon for the Giants. In the nineteenth century, owners typically ruled the roost, and from 1902 to 1932, manager John McGraw made virtually all baseball decisions for the Giants.

In 1946 Horace Stoneham hired his sister's son, Charles "Chub" Feeney, a graduate of Dartmouth and Fordham Law School. Feeney had his wedding reception at the Polo Grounds, and by 1950 he was vice president and general manager of the team. He went on to become president of the National League in 1969, and he held the line against bringing in the designated hitter.

Feeney helped engineer some of the Giants' greatest teams. After Stoneham hired Leo Durocher as manager, Feeney and Stoneham worked to shape the team in Durocher's image. They unloaded big boppers such as Walker Cooper and Johnny Mize and brought in Alvin Dark and Eddie Stanky, who helped win the pennant in 1951. In 1954 Feeney traded Bobby Thomson for Johnny Antonelli, who won 21 games for another pennant winner.

In San Francisco, a series of trades brought in Billy Pierce, Jack Sanford, Billy O'Dell, and Harvey Kuenn—key cogs on the 1962 pennant team. Trades of Felipe and Matty Alou and Orlando Cepeda, however, haunted the team in the 1960s.

Horace Stoneham stepped in as GM after Feeney left to become league president. When Stoneham put the team on the selling block, and put its fate in limbo, the National League assigned former Houston Astros GM Spec Richardson to take the Giants' job in 1976. While Richardson has been vilified in Houston for trading away the likes of Joe Morgan, he won Executive of the Year honors in San Francisco in 1978. A preseason trade to acquire Vida Blue from the A's helped turn a losing team into winners.

Following a four-year stint by former catcher Tom Haller, the GM job was given to Al Rosen, a stalwart on the 1954 Indians team that lost to the Giants in the World Series. After San Francisco lost 100 games in 1985, Rosen came in with manager Roger Craig and oversaw a transformation. Thanks to the promotion of rookies Will Clark and Robby Thompson, who never even played AAA baseball, the team showed some spark. In 1987 Rosen masterminded three midseason trades that brought Kevin Mitchell, Dave Dravecky, Rick Reuschel, and Don Robinson—and a division title. Rosen was named Executive of the Year, and two years later the Giants were in the World Series.

With new owners in 1993, veteran executive Bob Quinn became general manager. After winning a World Series with the

Al Rosen (left), with Roger Craig, October 1989

Brian Sabean, February 2008

Reds in 1990, Quinn could not lift the Giants to the next level, and he was replaced by his assistant, Brian Sabean, in 1996. Sabean has been loved and loathed by Giant fans during his tenure, but he earned their respect with his Midas-like moves that led to the 2010 title.

His biggest trade was unloading longtime fan favorite Matt Williams for Jeff Kent, Jose Vizcaino, and Julian Tavarez in 1996. Sabean was vilified at the time, but he defended the trade, asserting, "I am not an idiot." The GM was vindicated when Kent won the MVP Award in 2000 and was a key contributor on several postseason teams.

For much of his tenure, Sabean sought to maintain a capable veteran squad surrounding aging slugger Barry Bonds, bringing in the likes of Ellis Burks, Reggie Sanders, and Andres Gallaraga. The 2003 team won 100 games, and Sabean was named Executive of the Year.

Although he drove fans crazy by signing high-priced and underperforming veterans Aaron Rowand, Edgar Renteria, and Barry Zito, he also embraced the youth movement and refused to trade Tim Lincecum, Matt Cain, Jonathan Sanchez, and other young stars.

In 2010, Sabean's myriad moves helped win a pennant. He brought up Buster Posey in May and sent Bengie Molina to Texas. He shored up the bullpen with trades for Javier Lopez and Ramon Ramirez. He took other teams' castoffs in Pat Burrell, Aubrey Huff, Cody Ross, and Jose Guillen. The patchwork came together, and the Giants won it all.

THE TRADING POST

Christy Mathewson, in a Reds uniform, greeting John McGraw and Buck Herzog, July 1916

The trading block has been a major source of talent for the Giants over the years, as well as a source of controversy. The Giants have never shied away from trading a popular star—from Christy Mathewson to Willie Mays—when it suited their needs.

The Giants' first superstar was Buck Ewing, the greatest catcher of baseball's early era. Yet when John Montgomery Ward, a former teammate and Hall of Famer, became manager in 1893, he traded Ewing to the Cleveland Spiders for George Davis. Ewing nearly proved the trade a lemon by hitting .377, but Davis went on to hit .332 for the Giants over the next nine years on his way to the Hall of Fame.

Amos Rusie was a dominating pitcher in the 1890s, but he was also a frequent holdout, and injuries hastened his decline near the end of the decade. So, in December 1900, the Giants sent Rusie to Cincinnati in exchange for a young minor leaguer named Christy Mathewson.

Manager John McGraw was known for being devoted to his players, but he was even more devoted to winning. In mid-season 1916, when his beloved Matty's skills had declined, McGraw traded him to Cincinnati, along with Bill McKechnie and Edd Roush, for Buck Herzog and Red Killefer. While Mathewson appeared in only one game for the Reds before retiring, Edd Roush launched a Hall of Fame career in Cincinnati. Killefer batted 1.000 as a Giant—getting a hit in his only at bat with the team. Herzog

stayed through the 1917 pennant season but batted just .245 in a season and a half.

After the 1926 season, the Giants traded their biggest star, native New Yorker Frankie Frisch, still in his prime. McGraw had had a falling out with Frisch and sent him (and Jimmy Ring) to St. Louis for Rogers "Rajah" Hornsby in a swap of legends. Frisch went on to win an MVP Award and four pennants with the Cardinals; Hornsby batted .361 for New York in 1927 but then was shipped to the Boston Braves for catcher Shanty Hogan and journeyman Jimmy Welsh. Hogan proved to be a solid performer, but he was no Rajah.

Many Giants who were traded away often found their way back to the team. In 1938 manager Bill Terry swapped shortstop Dick Bartell, outfielder Hank Leiber, and catcher Gus Mancuso to the Cubs for counterparts Billy Jurges, Frank Demaree, and Ken O'Dea. (When a reporter asked what he thought of the trade, Terry replied with characteristic impatience, "What the hell do you think I think of it? I just made the trade!") By 1942 Bartell, Leiber, and Mancuso were all back playing for New York.

When the Giants returned to respectability in the 1950s, it was largely thanks to trades. Rival owner Bill Veeck hailed the acquisition of Alvin Dark and Eddie Stanky from the Boston Braves in exchange for Sid Gordon, Willard Marshall, Buddy Kerr, and Sam Webb as "one of the best trades in history."

Proving their lack of sentiment, the Giants sent Bobby Thomson—a hometown hero still beloved for his Dodger-killing home run—to Milwaukee in a six-player trade that brought pitcher Johnny Antonelli to New York in 1954. According to Veeck, Giant owner Horace Stoneham had pretended that Thomson's saintly status made him off limits, but he ultimately relented in order to obtain the promising Antonelli. Antonelli led the pennant-winning Giants with a 21–7 record in 1954, while Thomson never equaled his past glory.

Perhaps the most famous Giants trade was one that was never consummated: Dick Littlefield and $30,000 to Brooklyn for Jackie Robinson. Despite rumors of his refusal to report to the rival team, Robinson had already planned to retire and had taken a job with Chock Full o'Nuts. The trade was voided.

The Giants rebuilt in the late 1950s, largely with farmhands such as Willie McCovey and Orlando Cepeda, but they also acquired some key pitching help via trades. In 1958 they sent Ruben Gomez to the Phillies for Jack Sanford and a year later traded outfielder Jackie Brandt to the Orioles for Billy O'Dell. In 1961 the Giants shipped four prospects (who never panned out) to the White Sox for Billy Pierce and Don Larsen. Thus the Giants built their pennant-winning pitching staff of 1962.

Trades in the ensuing years were not so kind to the Giants. Matty Alou was traded to Pittsburgh for Joe Gibbon and Ozzie Virgil in 1965. Alou won a batting title for the Pirates in 1966.

The team always had trouble making room for two first basemen, McCovey and Cepeda, so in 1966 the Baby Bull was shipped to the Cardinals for pitcher Ray Sadecki. Sadecki never came close to his 20-win season of 1964, while Cepeda won an MVP Award and World Series in 1967.

The Giants dealt promising farmhand George Foster to Cincinnati in 1971, without getting much in return; Foster became a key slugger on the Big Red Machine. Giants infielder Tito Fuentes grumbled that the move was typical of the era: "They said he wasn't a good player, but he went to Cincinnati, and someone taught him how to hit the curveball. The Giants didn't take the time to work with young players."

After finally reaching the postseason in 1971, the Giants began shedding old heroes. That winter Gaylord Perry was traded to the Indians for Sam McDowell. (Perry won the Cy Young Award the next year and still had 180 wins left in his spitball.) The aging Willie Mays was traded to the New York Mets in 1972. In 1973 Juan Marichal was sold to the Red Sox, and Willie McCovey was traded to the Padres.

In the 1980s the Giants rebuilt their batting order through the draft and their pitching staff through trades, acquiring veterans Mike Krukow, Rick Reuschel, and Don Robinson.

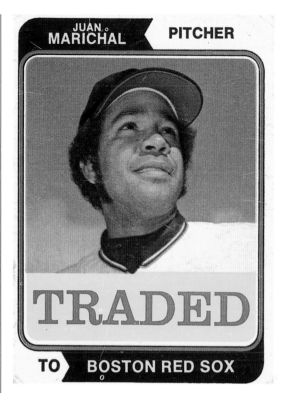

Juan Marichal, 1974 Topps baseball card

Willie Mays, with Mayor John Lindsay, May 1972

When Brian Sabean became general manager, he acted boldly, angering Giant fans by trading the beloved Matt Williams for Jeff Kent and two others. Kent went on to form a fearsome tandem with Barry Bonds in San Francisco, and Sabean was hailed as a genius. Sabean became particularly adept at making deadline deals to juice the Giants through pennant races, such as the acquisition of Kirk Rueter in 1996, Wilson Alvarez and Roberto Hernandez in 1997, and Jason Schmidt in 2001.

Sabean also continued to draw fans' ire, however, with some questionable moves. Perhaps the worst trade in recent years saw the Giants send promising pitchers Joe Nathan, Francisco Liriano, and Boof Bonser to the Twins for catcher A. J. Pierzynski in 2003. While Nathan became an all-star closer, Pierzynski brought dissension to the clubhouse and was released at the end of the year.

The 2010 Giants were built mostly from the farm system and through free agency, with only Freddy Sanchez arriving through a major trade, acquired from Pittsburgh in 2009 for prospect Tim Alderson. But as the season wore on, Sabean went shopping. He sent Bengie Molina to Texas for reliever Chris Ray, prospect Daniel Turpen to the Red Sox for reliever Ramon Ramirez, and John Bowker and Joe Martinez to Pittsburgh for reliever Javier Lopez—building one of the best bullpens in baseball and a key to the team's eventual title.

Joe Nathan, October 2003

A. J. Pierzynski, July 2004

GIANT CHARACTERS

Mike Donlin honored at Polo Grounds, 1911

While the Giants can boast that the team has suited up more Hall of Famers than any other franchise, the all-time roster also includes its share of baseball's clowns and colorful characters. When John McGraw ran the club, baseball was a rough-and-tumble game, and McGraw one of its foremost tough guys. Not surprisingly, he valued the same type of hard-nosed player. He had one in "Turkey" Mike Donlin. The nickname, given for his strut, also fit his ill-advised behavior. A hard-drinking, hard-fighting man, Donlin first played for McGraw in Baltimore and then on several pennant winners in New York, hitting .333 for his career. Twice he quit baseball for vaudeville, twice he married actresses, and many more times than that he was arrested.

One Giant became famous accidentally, and posthumously, for barely having that proverbial big league cup of coffee. Archibald "Moonlight" Graham played two innings in an 11–1 win for the 1905 Giants, never even coming to bat. He left the game and became a doctor in Minnesota. Sound familiar? Nearly a century later, he was immortalized in the classic 1989 film *Field of Dreams*, with Burt Lancaster playing the aged Dr. Moonlight Graham.

Journeyman Eddie Grant, a Giant from 1913 to 1915, became the only major league baseball player to die in World War I, and the Giants honored him with a plaque in center field at the Polo Grounds. When some suggested the "Curse of Captain Eddie" haunted the Giants in San Francisco, the team commissioned a replica of the plaque.

The strangest character of the McGraw era had to be Charles "Victory" Faust, a Kansas farmhand who joined the team in 1911. He claimed that a fortune teller had told him that if he pitched for the Giants, the team would win the World Series. Although McGraw quickly saw that Faust had no athletic talent, he became a mascot and traveled with the team. After the Giants clinched the pennant that year, McGraw even let him get in a game. The prophesy went only so far, however, and the Giants lost the World Series. Faust's career was over.

The great Native American athlete Jim Thorpe played six years for the Giants. He was with the 1917 pennant winners and was written in McGraw's starting lineup for one series game but was replaced in the first inning and never actually played.

After Babe Ruth's Yankees moved to a new baseball palace across the river from the Polo Grounds in 1923, it drove McGraw crazy that the Yanks were outdrawing his team in attendance. In response, he decided to bring in a Jewish star, since the population of New York was one-quarter Jewish at the time.

Mose Solomon was tearing up the minors in 1923, belting 49 homers for a Kansas farm club. McGraw and company knew that he couldn't do the same in the bigs, but they brought him up just the same, exploiting his moniker, "the Rabbi of Swat." Fans came out, but McGraw didn't play him until the end of the season. A first baseman, Solomon had Hall of Famers George Kelly and Bill Terry ahead of him. He went 3 for 8 in two games, then back to the minors, never to return.

Casey Stengel, led off field after scuffle against Phillies, 1923

Jack "Lucky" Lohrke (right), with Nicholas Witek, February 1947

In the 1923 World Series, the most notable player for the Giants in a losing effort against the Yankees was reserve outfielder Casey Stengel. With Game One tied 4–4 in the bottom of the ninth, Stengel—on an injured leg—hit an inside-the-park home run, losing a shoe on his way around the bases. In Game Three, Stengel hit one out of the park, keying a 1–0 Giant win. Those were the only games the Giants won, and McGraw traded Stengel to the Braves after the season. The "Old Perfessor" later quipped, "It's a good thing I didn't hit three homers in three games, or McGraw would have traded me to the Three-I League!"

Jack "Lucky" Lohrke brought an amazing backstory to his arrival on the 1947 Giants. Lohrke had earned his nickname: he had survived the Battle of the Bulge, while four soldiers on either side of him were killed in combat in one day. Another time, a higher ranking officer bumped him from a plane he was going to take home from the war; the plane crashed, killing all aboard. Once home and playing minor league baseball, he got the call for a promotion to join the AAA team. He hitchhiked home while his teammates took the bus to their next game; the bus plunged off a mountain pass, killing nine. Lohrke died in 2009 at age 85.

Leo Durocher loved Dusty Rhodes for his bat but feared the damage he could do in the field. "I ain't much of a fielder and I got a pretty lousy arm, but I sure love to whack at that ball," Rhodes himself said in a 1954 interview. That year, Rhodes proved it in the World Series, going four for six with 7 RBI and hitting home runs off Hall of Famers Bob Lemon and Early Wynn. He didn't even play Game Four. "It was just as well," he said later. "After the third game I was drinking to everybody's health so much that I about ruined mine."

Jeffrey "Hac-Man" Leonard was an intense presence on the Giants teams of the 1980s, transforming himself several times over: from Jeff to Jeffrey, from spray hitter to slugger, from uniform numbers 20 and 26 to his distinctive 00. Opponents hated his "one flap down" home-run trot, accomplished with one arm dangling at his side. Though he clashed with teammate Will Clark, Leonard homered in four straight games in the 1987 NLCS, winning the MVP for the series, which the Giants lost.

When the Giants made Rod Beck the closer in 1992, a new fan favorite was born. Here was "Shooter," a beer-guzzling ballplayer, listed at 6-foot-1 and 235 pounds, who looked like he'd be more comfortable at a tailgate party than out on the mound. But glaring out from above his Fu Manchu mustache, Beck was a dominant reliever, saving 199 games in seven seasons. When he died at age 38 in 2007, the Giants wore his number 47 on an armband the rest of the year.

Dusty Rhodes (left), with Leo Durocher, July 1952

Below left: *Jeffrey "Hac-Man" Leonard, 1987 NLCS*

Below right: *Rod Beck (center), with Barry Bonds, celebrating division title, September 1997*

John Montgomery Ward, newspaper illustration, November 1888

I n the 1880s, by the time John B. Day had established the Giants in the National League, baseball owners had already implemented the reserve clause, putting in every contract the rule that effectively bound a player to a team for life—and if the player didn't like it, he could seek another profession.

Ballplayers weren't paid particularly well, and they were frequently sold from one team to another. Players sometimes got other perks, however. Stockbrokers who attended Giants games so appreciated star Roger Connor, the most prolific home-run hitter of the era, that they took up a collection after one particularly long blast and bought him a gold watch from Tiffany's.

In 1889 John T. Brush got the league to approve a plan by which owners would rate players from A to E. The grades would be based on both ability and morality, and salaries would range from $1,500 for an E player to $2,500 for an A player.

Unfortunately for Brush, one of his stars, John Montgomery Ward, earned a law degree in 1885 and helped start a players' union. Ward protested the new plan but got nowhere, so in 1890 he started a breakaway league that was more favorable to players, taking many Giants stars with him. The league lasted only a year, however, and when it ended, Buck Ewing returned as the highest paid Giant, earning a salary of $5,500. The owners continued to hold the power for nearly a century after that.

In 1908, when Fred Snodgrass earned a spot in the big leagues, the Giants paid him $150 a month. In 1912 Snodgrass made an error that many felt cost the Giants the World Series, but McGraw remembered his great catch on the next play and gave him a $1,000 raise in 1913.

Bill Terry, known for his financial acumen, often antagonized McGraw by holding out in the spring. In 1931 the holdout ended badly, and Terry took a $5,000 cut in pay from his 1930 salary of $23,000—presumably because his batting average had dropped 52 points, from .401 to .349. (Also presumably, any other .349 hitter would get a raise.)

In 1957, speaking with writer Sid Gray, Carl Hubbell recalled his contract negotiation upon arriving with the Giants in 1928. When it came time to discuss salary, Hubbell timidly asked for $750 a month, $350 more than he received in the minors. McGraw said, "Okay," and Hubbell thought he had become "the richest man in the world."

Rookies were always something of a bargain. When Orlando Cepeda reported to San Francisco in 1958, he didn't even have a contract; 10 minutes before game time, he signed for $7,000. In June, when he was tearing the cover off the ball, he got a raise to $9,500. After the season, when he was Rookie of the Year, the Giants offered $12,000; Cepeda asked for $20,000, which was one-third of what the Giants were paying Willie Mays, who had had a comparable year. He settled for $17,000, but his contract negotiations were always a battle. In 1961, after hitting .311 and leading the league with 46 home runs and 142 RBI, Cepeda sought a $20,000 raise, to $50,000. He made it to $46,000.

Mays earned $85,000 in 1961. That rose to $90,000 the next year and in 1963 to $105,000—"the highest, I was told, ever paid a ballplayer in straight salary," Mays later wrote.

Barry Zito, with Brian Sabean, January 2007

In 1975 the reserve clause was eliminated after a long and hard-fought battle by the players' union. The era of free agency was at hand. The Giants' biggest free-agent splash came in 1993, when they signed Barry Bonds to a six-year, $43.75 million salary. Bonds was not only San Francisco royalty but had already won two MVP awards with Pittsburgh. In January 2002, after he broke the single-season home run record, the Giants re-signed him for five years and $90 million.

Not every free agent has been as successful. Before the 2005 season, the Giants signed Armando Benitez for three years and $21 million, but injuries helped make the closer a giant bust. Fans continue to debate the 2007 signing of Barry Zito for seven years and $126 million, the most any pitcher had ever been paid at the time. Zito has not recaptured the Cy Young form he showed with the Oakland A's, but he's proven durable and a good mentor to the Giants' young arms.

While the Giants have paid some of their homegrown stars—Tim Lincecum signed a two-year, $23 million contract in 2010, and Matt Cain got a similar deal—they also built the championship squad with low-budget castoffs. With their new rings, however, some of that talent got more expensive. Aubrey Huff, who made $3 million in 2010, signed a two-year, $22 million deal, and the team's payroll moved past $100 million for the first time in 2011.

GIANT MANAGERS

In his ever-present top hat, Jim Mutrie was a nineteenth-century dandy. He wasn't the Giants' first manager—that honor goes to John Clapp, who held the job for the inaugural 1883 season—but Mutrie gave the team its name when he, with characteristic enthusiasm, proclaimed, "My big fellows! My Giants!" He served as skipper from 1885 to 1891 and led the team to its first championships, in 1888 and 1889.

While more than three dozen men have held the reins as manager of the Giants, the words *Giant* and *manager* will forever conjure up one man: John "Muggsy" McGraw. In the words of the great Connie Mack, whose Athletics were frequent World Series foes of the Giants, "There has been only one manager, and his name is John McGraw." Less flatteringly was this assessment from McGraw's own coach, Arlie Latham: "McGraw eats gunpowder every morning and washes it down with warm blood."

Fiercely competitive, McGraw fought with nearly everyone, yet he was revered for his devotion to his own players and for being a brilliant tactician. He excelled at what was known in his day as inside baseball and today as small ball: bunts, hit-and-run, stolen bases, and aggressive base running. Until his championship teams of the 1920s, McGraw rarely had a Hall of Fame position player (catcher Roger Bresnahan being the only one) and relied on pitching, defense, and speed to scratch out runs and win games. In 31 years with the Giants, he accumulated a record of 2,583 wins and 1,790 losses (a .591 winning percentage) while winning 10 National League pennants and three World Series.

Forty games into the 1932 season, McGraw handed the reins to the team's biggest star, Bill Terry. Not only was Terry a Hall of Fame–caliber player, but as manager in the 1930s he took the Giants to three World Series, including a championship in 1933, while also batting .322 as the team's first baseman.

Jim Mutrie, 1888

John McGraw, 1911

Leo Durocher, circa 1948

Bill Rigney, 1960

Terry had inherited McGraw's passion for winning, but when he passed the team to his big star, Mel Ott, the Giants' fortunes faded. Leo Durocher was the manager of the rival Brooklyn Dodgers in 1946 when he offered up this remark: "Do you know a nicer guy in the world than Mel Ott? He's a nice guy. In last place. Where am I? In first place. . . . The nice guys are over there in last place."

Headline writers ultimately edited those remarks into Durocher's calling card: "Nice guys finish last." Durocher parlayed that combativeness into his own greatest success in baseball, as manager of the New York Giants.

Giants fans, naturally, were mortified when their biggest foe came crosstown to manage the team in 1948. But by 1951 Durocher had delivered the franchise's first pennant in 14 years, and in 1954 the team won the World Series. "I come to beat you," Durocher wrote in his autobiography. "I come to kill you." John McGraw would have been proud.

Durocher's successor, Bill Rigney, was a class act. He led the Giants as they moved west but could not lead them to the promised land of a title. Rigney snapped a 54-year run in which the Giants were managed by Hall of Famers. A Durocher protégé and former Giants star, Alvin Dark took over as manager in 1961 and led the team to a pennant the following year. Devoutly religious, Dark was also fiercely competitive. He has been called the most controversial manager in San Francisco history for his system of rating players, for racially insensitive remarks, and for watering the base paths to slow down Dodgers speedster Maury Wills.

When Dark couldn't get the Giants back to the series, owner Horace Stoneham replaced him with Herman Franks. Franks barely had better luck. With a roster boasting several Hall of Famers in their prime (Willie Mays, Willie McCovey, Juan Marichal, Orlando Cepeda, and Gaylord Perry), Franks led the team to four consecutive second-place finishes from 1965 to 1968 before finally resigning in frustration. Upon Franks' resignation, Bob Stevens wrote in the *San Francisco Chronicle*, "He simply had the outrageous misfortune to manage when Sandy Koufax pitched for the Dodgers and Bob Gibson for the Cardinals." Franks' successor, Clyde King, also led the Giants to a second-place finish in 1969.

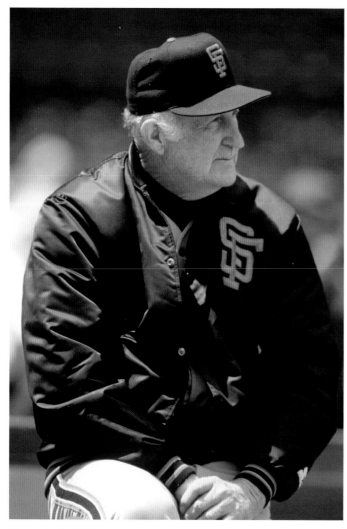

Roger Craig, 1992

Dusty Baker, 2002 World Series

With the advent of divisional play, the Giants finally reached the postseason in 1971, "the Year of the Fox," so named for manager Charlie Fox. Fox fell victim to some bad trades, and the team fell into a spiral, never finishing higher than third place over the next 15 years. Between 1968 and 1986, the Giants went through 11 managers, including Rigney for a return stint, and had a rare winning season in 1978, when Joe Altobelli was named Manager of the Year. Things fizzled the next year, however, and he was replaced.

In 1981 owner Bob Lurie made Frank Robinson the first African American to manage in both leagues. He led the Giants to their first back-to-back winning seasons in a decade.

That turnaround was not sustained, however, until Roger Craig—a former pitcher and longtime coach—took over near the end of the 1985 season. With Craig's rallying cry of "Humm Baby," the Giants went on a tear of five straight winning seasons, with a division title in 1987 and a National League pennant in 1989.

New owners brought in an old Dodger, Dusty Baker, to manage the club beginning in 1993. Thanks to a lineup featuring Barry Bonds, Baker became the winningest skipper in San Francisco history, eclipsing Craig; he is second to only McGraw in both cities. (Baker left San Francisco a mere 1,743 wins shy of McGraw's mark.) Popular with players and fans, the easygoing Baker led the team to 103 wins in his first season but fell just shy of the playoffs. He had them in contention through most of his tenure, capturing division titles in 1997 and 2000. Ninety-five wins and a wild card berth in 2002 culminated in a trip to the World Series.

Among the most enduring images of that series are Baker's three-year-old son, Darren, a batboy, running out to home plate and almost getting steamrolled by an oncoming base runner, and quick-thinking J. T. Snow grabbing him by the collar and whisking him to safety. A less pleasant image is Baker taking the game ball from Russ Ortiz, as he removed the pitcher from Game Six

Felipe Alou, 2006

Bruce Bochy, 2009

with a 5–0 lead and eight outs to go for a Giants' championship, only to watch as the bullpen unraveled.

By then Baker was clashing with managing general partner Peter Magowan, and he was fired after the World Series. Baker was replaced by a Giants legend, Felipe Alou, who had once played alongside his brothers Matty and Jesus in the Giants' outfield and had managed his son Moises with the Expos in the 1990s—and did so again with the Giants in 2005 and 2006. The elder Alou led the Giants to 100 wins and another division title in 2003, followed by a near miss in 2004. After two winning seasons, however, he could not stave off Bonds' decline, and the team suffered two losing seasons.

The Giants knew Bruce Bochy was a winner when they hired him from the San Diego Padres in 2007, but he became a Giants legend in 2010, masterfully juggling a lineup that struggled with injuries and battled to score runs. He lovingly called his players castoffs and misfits; other teams had rejected the likes of Aubrey Huff, Andres Torres, Pat Burrell, and Cody Ross, but they found success with Bochy's Giants. The manager convinced his players to accept their roles, and he continued to tinker with the batting order well into the postseason. His artful use of the bullpen and his magic touch with hitters led to a championship, and his low-key approach earned admiration among players and fans.

Monte Irvin, Willie Mays, and Hank Thompson, 1951

THE RACE BARRIER

Baseball's great shame and tragedy remains the color line, drawn by team owners in the nineteenth century and extended for more than 50 years. The Brooklyn Dodgers and Branch Rickey finally broke it, installing Jackie Robinson in the infield in 1947, where he won Rookie of the Year honors.

With the Dodgers' groundbreaking move, the Giants were not far behind, and they didn't have to look far. The Negro League team in nearby Newark, New Jersey, the Eagles, featured two top stars. Many believed that one of them, Monte Irvin, would be the player to break the color line. The Dodgers even signed Irvin to a contract, but when Eagles owner Effa Manley demanded compensation, Rickey voided the deal. The Giants swooped in and signed Irvin and teammate Hank Thompson before the 1949 season, assigning them to the minor league affiliate in Jersey City. Irvin and Thompson joined the Giants on July 5 and played in their first game on July 8. (Thompson had previously integrated the St. Louis Browns, in 1947, before joining the Giants' farm system.)

Irvin said that putting on the Giants uniform was "one of the greatest thrills of my life." He had been a star in segregated baseball for years, winning a batting title and championship in the

Frank Robinson, 1982

Masanori Murakami, 1964

Tsuyoshi Shinjo, 2002 World Series

Negro Leagues. "I thought about the long road that I had traveled to get there," he wrote in his autobiography, "and the fact that it was finally happening was a feeling that is indescribable."

Irvin recounted how manager Leo Durocher addressed the team upon his arrival: "If you're green or purple or whatever color, you can play for me if I think you can help this ballclub. That's all I'm going to say about race."

"After that, we felt great," Irvin wrote. "I know that Jackie had some trouble with the Dodgers, but we never had any problem on the Giants."

On July 8, 1949, when Thompson came to bat against the Dodgers' Don Newcombe, it marked the first time a black pitcher faced a black batter in a major league game.

The Dodgers also nearly signed another Negro Leaguer, but they decided that 16-year-old Willie Mays of the Birmingham Black Barons couldn't hit a curveball, and he remained unsigned. By 1950 Mays had learned to hit the curve, and the Giants signed him. After batting .477 in 35 games with the Minneapolis Millers, Mays was called up to the big league club in May 1951. He joined Irvin and Thompson to form the first all-black outfield, and the trio was key in the team's run for the pennant that year.

Thirty years later, the Giants continued to break ground when they hired Frank Robinson as manager. Robinson had been the first black manager in Major League Baseball when he led the Indians in 1975. When the Giants hired him in 1981, he became the National League's first African American manager. Dusty Baker managed the team from 1993 to 2002, winning 840 games (second in Giants' history only to John McGraw), two Manager of the Year awards, and one National League pennant.

The San Francisco Giants, from their perch on the Pacific Rim, also led the way in expanding baseball's reach across the globe. They made baseball history in 1964 when they signed pitcher Masanori Murakami, the first Japanese-born player in the major leagues. The lefty reliever had a 5–1 record and 3.43 ERA in just over a season with the Giants. In 2002 Giants outfielder Tsuyoshi Shinjo became the first Japanese player to play in the World Series.

LATIN PLAYERS

Light-skinned Latin American ballplayers managed to play in the major leagues for years before Jackie Robinson broke the color line for African Americans. Among the most famous was Cuban pitcher Adolfo Luque, who came up with the Boston Braves in 1914 and later pitched for the Cincinnati Reds in the 1919 World Series. "The Pride of Havana" faced plenty of racial epithets, and he once charged the Giants' bench and socked Casey Stengel in the jaw.

Luque finished his career in a Giants uniform. At age 42, he threw 4⅓ innings of scoreless relief to pick up the win in the deciding game of the 1933 World Series.

Baseball's integration in 1947 opened the door for Latinos of all colors. The Giants had a leg up, because Alex Pompez, the flamboyant owner of the Negro Leagues' New York Cubans, had an arrangement with Horace Stoneham to use the Polo Grounds when the Giants were out of town. (Willie Mays made his Polo Grounds debut in a game against the Cubans in 1948.) When the Negro National League folded in 1950, Pompez became a scout for the Giants.

In 1953 the Giants signed Puerto Rican pitcher Ruben Gomez, and he went 17–9 for the 1954 pennant winners. Schools closed in Puerto Rico to allow students to watch Gomez pitch in the World Series that year; he won Game Three. When Gomez returned to San Juan after the series, he was greeted by 5,000 fans in the rain, and the governor declared a holiday.

Gomez also had the distinction of winning the first major league game on the West Coast, in 1958.

By the time the team arrived in San Francisco, the Giants were stocked with great Latin players. Pompez had hired his old all-star shortstop Horacio Martinez as a scout in the Dominican Republic, where he found the three Alou brothers—Felipe, Matty,

Adolfo Luque, October 1933

Jesus, Matty, and Felipe Alou, September 1963

and Jesus—as well as Manny Mota and Juan Marichal, "the Dominican Dandy."

In a 2003 interview with the *San Francisco Chronicle* after he
was hired as Giants manager, Alou recalled the racism he faced in
his early playing days. Assigned to a minor league team in Lake
Charles, Louisiana, in 1956, he had to leave after only nine at bats
because the community prohibited blacks from playing on the
same field as whites.

Later, he had to fight more subtle stereotypes. "The percep-
tion of almost every Latin was that he was a hot dog, a showoff,
or he doesn't play hard or hustle," Alou told Henry Schulman.
"We were surrounded by all of those things. . . . It made us
uncomfortable. I wouldn't say angry, but there were some things
inside every one of us."

In the early 1960s, the Puerto Rican–born Orlando Cepeda
clashed with manager Alvin Dark, who at one point ordered
players not to speak Spanish in the clubhouse.

Tito Fuentes, a Cuban infielder, was told that the Giants
would sign him for bonus money only if he were white. "I
said, 'That's going to be hard for me to do,'" Fuentes recalled.
He ultimately did sign, in 1962, and spent nine years with the
team. He still serves as a Spanish-language broadcaster for
Giants games.

In 2005, when Felipe Alou managed the Giants, a talk radio
host blasted the team's "brain-dead Caribbean hitters hacking
at slop nightly." The Giants' lineup at the time included Ven-
ezuelans Omar Vizquel and Edgardo Alfonzo and Dominicans
Pedro Feliz and Deivi Cruz. Alou retorted with an angry con-
demnation. "I never heard of anything like that here [in San
Francisco]," Alou said. "I heard [it] in the South and some other
cities, but not here. It tells me that a man like me and the Latin
guys have to be aware it's not over yet, or it is coming back."
The radio host was fired.

The 2010 champion Giants featured many Latino stars. Edgar
Renteria of Colombia won the World Series MVP, Dominican
Juan Uribe played all over the infield and was second on the team
in RBIs, Venezuelan Pablo Sandoval started at third, and Puerto
Rican Andres Torres starred in center field. Jonathan Sanchez
of Mayaguez, Puerto Rico, who on July 10, 2009, became the
first Giants pitcher in more than 30 years to throw a no-hitter,
was stellar on the mound in 2010, while Javier Lopez, Ramon
Ramirez, and Santiago Casilla were linchpins of the bullpen.
Freddy Sanchez—a Southern Californian of Mexican descent—
played solid second base and hit .292.

Omar Vizquel and Pedro Feliz, September 2007

Pablo Sandoval and Bengie Molina, June 2009

NICKNAMES

Baseball players used to need nicknames like they needed gloves and bats. Getting a nickname was almost a rite of passage.

From the first Gothams team—featuring Dasher Troy, Buck Ewing, Tip O'Neill, and Smiling Mickey Welch—the Giants have featured some of baseball's most evocative nicknames.

John McGraw hated to be called Muggsy, which came from his Baltimore days—it referred to either a ward boss or a comic strip tramp from that city—but he loved his sobriquet of Little Napoleon. At 5-foot-6 and dictatorial in nature, he fit the name.

The origins of other nicknames are harder to nail down. No one can explain definitively why Christy Mathewson was known as Big Six, although several explanations exist. One theory is that it stemmed from his height—he stood 6-feet, unusually tall in those days. The Matheson Motor Company made a "peerless" car known as Big Six, and a local fire engine also had that nickname. Perhaps Matty (as he was more widely called) pumped like Big

Six. Years later, McGraw claimed credit. He said one day when New York Typographical Union No. 6 won a big settlement, he was asked who was pitching and replied, "Let's put in Big Six."

Bix Six's mound-mate, Joe McGinnity, earned his "Iron Man" nickname not merely for lasting so many innings but also because he worked in his father-in-law's iron mill.

Nicknames in those days weren't always the hallmark of sensitivity. Luther Taylor, who was deaf and could not speak, became Dummy. (The Giants learned sign language to communicate with him, which some say was the birth of baseball's hand signals.) John "Chief" Meyers was a Cahuilla Indian. Country folks were routinely called Rube, although you couldn't always count on that connection. The great Rube Marquard was from Cleveland; he got the nickname in the minor leagues, when fans thought he resembled established star Rube Waddell.

Dave "Beauty" Bancroft wasn't particularly pretty. *New York Herald* sportswriter Dan Daniel recalled that when Bancroft arrived in the majors with the Phillies in 1915, "he brought with him a habit of shouting 'Beauty' every time his pitcher sent over a good-looking ball. That's the history of the 'Beauty' handle."

Native New Yorker Frankie Frisch's choice of college couldn't have led to any nickname other than the "Fordham Flash." When the Giants were royalty in the 1930s, alliteration coronated King Carl Hubbell, and it was only natural that the next great pitcher to come up would be Prince Hal Schumacher. Hubbell was also the "Meal Ticket"; when he took the mound, it was money in the bank.

Memphis Bill Terry starred and then managed those teams, followed by "Master Melvin" Ott, who did the same. Ott gave way to one of the most aptly nicknamed managers ever: Leo "the Lip" Durocher.

Durocher's greatest star, Willie Mays, was known to his teammates as Buck but was known to fans and sportswriters as the Say Hey Kid, another nickname with unclear origins. *New York Journal American* writer Barney Kremenko said the rookie Mays "would blurt 'Say who,' 'Say what,' 'Say where,' 'Say hey.' In my paper, I tabbed him the 'Say Hey Kid.' It stuck." Mays claimed that sportswriter Jimmy Cannon coined it. "You see a guy, you say, 'Hey, man. Say hey, man,'" Mays said in 2006. "Ted was the 'Splinter.' Joe was 'Joltin' Joe.' Stan was 'The Man.'

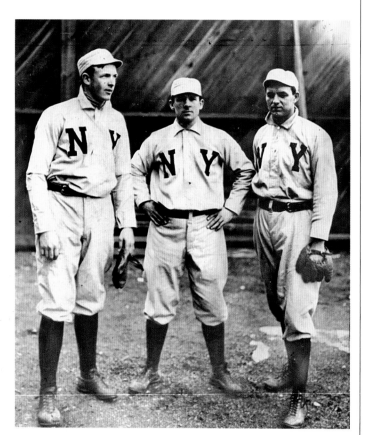

Big Six, Muggsy, and Iron Man, 1905

Chief Meyers (left), with Chief Bender, 1911 World Series

Say Hey Kid, Dominican Dandy, and Stretch, 1970

I guess I hit a few home runs, and they said there goes the 'Say Hey Kid.'"

When Mays first got to San Francisco, he found help in the lineup from Orlando "Baby Bull" Cepeda, and they were joined the next year by Willie "Stretch" McCovey. The arrival of "Dominican Dandy" Juan Marichal added to a Hall of Fame roster.

Scribes say that nicknames became a dying art in baseball around this time. Frank Deford blames television, "the utter visualization of sport at the expense of imagination." Still, the Giants have a long, proud history of nicknames, from at least 19 guys named Red and 10 named Lefty to creative 1970s monikers such as Dirty Al Gallagher (who refused to change his uniform during a 24-game collegiate hitting streak), John "the Count" Montefusco, and Dave "Kong" Kingman, among others.

The Giants of the 1980s had an edible outfield of Chili Davis and Candy Maldonado, and at first base installed Will "the Thrill" Clark. Clark's answering machine once made its message clear, playing B. B. King's "The Thrill Is Gone." On the mound, who wanted to face Don "Caveman" Robinson or Rick "Big Daddy" Reuschel?

Perhaps the curmudgeons are right. No one ever really tagged Barry Bonds with a nickname. But when the cover of *Sports Illustrated* anoints Tim Lincecum "the Freak," and when Barry Zito watches roly-poly teammate Pablo Sandoval leap

Captain Quirk and the Freak, 2009

over a catcher to score and dubs him "Kung Fu Panda," hope for a new generation of nicknames remains alive. Zito himself was known as a bit of a freak in his early days, earning the nickname "Captain Quirk." "Pat the Bat" Burrell, "Andres the Giant" Torres, and Aubrey "Huff Daddy" Huff added to the lovability of the 2010 club.

Fred Merkle, Larry Doyle, Christy Mathewson, John McGraw, and Fred Snodgrass, 1911

ROOKIES

Is there anything better, or worse, than being a major league rookie? Every major leaguer has experienced the thrill of walking into a clubhouse for the first time, putting on the uniform, and stepping onto a big league field. Yet many have also learned the indignities of the rookie experience, when the veterans put them in their place.

"It was practically impossible for a youngster, a rookie, to get up to the plate in batting practice," Fred Snodgrass recalled of his maiden season in 1908. "A youngster was an outsider, and those old veterans weren't about to make it easy for him to take away one of their jobs."

That year, Snodgrass saw what else could go wrong for rookies when 19-year-old Fred Merkle failed to step on second base in a crucial game and was called out. Teammate Larry Doyle, also playing his first full season in 1908, finished third in the National League that season with a .308 batting average.

Christy Mathewson was clearly something special right out of the gate, starting 38 games in his first year, 1901, finishing 36

of them, and winning 20 with 221 strikeouts. Several other Giant rookies have notched 20-win seasons over the years, including Cliff Melton in 1937, Bill Voiselle in 1944 (he actually won 21), and Larry Jansen in 1947.

Only one Giants rookie has lost 20 games in a season. In 1899 "Doughnut Bill" Carrick had the kind of debut not likely to be seen again. He set rookie records for starts (43) and hits allowed (485) while posting a 16–27 record with 40 complete games and 361 2/3 innings pitched. He also hit 23 batters.

Rookie outfielder Josh Devore hit .304 for the 1910 Giants and never hit .300 again. First-year pitcher Jeff Tesreau was 17–7 with a league-leading 1.96 ERA for McGraw's 1912 pennant winners. He lost his first game due to three errors, but the *New York Times* wrote of the outing, "Tesreau has curves which bend like barrel hoops and speed like lightning. He's just the kind of a strong man McGraw has been looking for."

Ah, the promise of rookies. Slick Castleman never had another year like 1935, when he went 15–6 for Bill Terry's

Giants. Babe Young managed to follow up his 101-RBI rookie year of 1940 with similar numbers in 1941, but he tailed off after that, hastened by a three-year hiatus in the military.

Sometimes you can tell a good player right from the start. In 1947 Bobby Thomson hit .283, with 29 home runs, 85 RBI, and 105 runs scored. Even though he's remembered best for that one home run, the Flying Scot had a 15-year career with 264 home runs and a lifetime .270 average.

Willie Mays started out hitless in his first 12 at bats. He broke the ice with a home run off Warren Spahn on May 28, 1951, but then went on another 0-for-13 slide. "Mister Leo," he cried to manager Durocher, "I can't hit up here." Durocher told Mays he was sticking with him, Mays found his confidence and his stroke, and he was on his way. He hit .274 with 20 home runs and was named Rookie of the Year (an award first handed out in 1947).

Hoyt Wilhelm debuted in 1952, a 28-year-old knuckle-baller in an era before baseball had defined relief specialists. He was 15–3 that year, all in relief, and led the league with a 2.43 ERA, 71 games, and an .833 winning percentage, the third best percentage ever by a rookie pitcher with at least 15 wins.

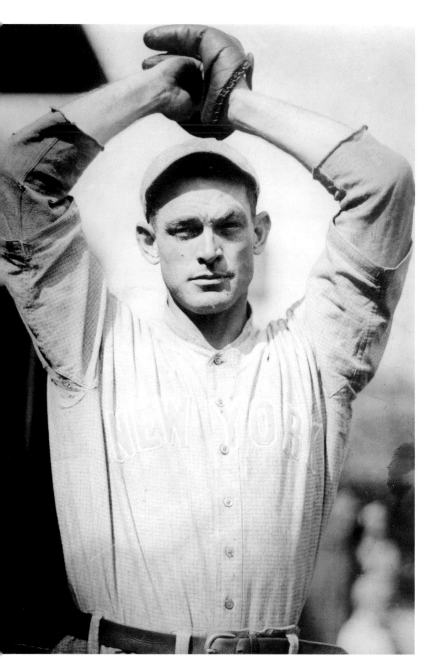

Jeff Tesreau, circa 1912

Hoyt Wilhelm, 1952

Orlando Cepeda, circa 1958

Willie McCovey, with 1959 Rookie of the Year trophy

When the Giants arrived in San Francisco in 1958, they had a farm system stocked with talent. Orlando Cepeda came up that year and immediately endeared himself to fans by cracking a home run in his debut—the first major league game on the West Coast, in which the Giants beat the Dodgers 8–0 at Seals Stadium. Cepeda won Rookie of the Year honors, hitting .312 with 25 home runs and 96 RBI.

The next year, Willie McCovey came up in midseason, went 4 for 4 against Hall of Famer Robin Roberts, and won Rookie of the Year honors, hitting .354 with 13 home runs in only 52 games. His season included a 22-game hitting streak.

Impressive debuts in the 1960s included Jim Ray Hart's 31 homers in 1964 and Frank Linzy's 9–3 record with a 1.43 ERA in 1965.

In the 1970s, Giants took home a pair of prizes. Gary Matthews won Rookie of the Year honors in 1973 with a .300 average. Two years later, John "the Count" Montefusco burst on the scene with a 15–9 record, a 2.88 ERA, 215 strikeouts—and another Rookie of the Year Award for the Giants.

In the "Humm Baby" 1986 season, the Giants debuted another impressive pair. Second sacker Robby Thompson batted .272 and was a Rookie of the Year runner-up, while 22-year-old first baseman Will Clark hit .287 and got everyone's attention with a home run in his first at bat, off none other than Nolan Ryan.

In the Barry Bonds era, the Giants built more through acquisition than promotion. Still, some newbies broke in in big ways. In 2004, 30-year-old rookie Brian Dallimore finally got the call to the big leagues; his first hit was a grand slam home run. His career lasted all of 27 games.

Big crowds turned out on August 29, 2005, and May 6, 2007, to see the Giants roll out the future: Matt Cain and Tim Lincecum, respectively. Cain was impressive in seven starts that debut year, and in his official rookie year in 2006, he whiffed 179 batters in 157 innings. Lincecum struck out 150 batters in 146 innings in his first season.

Thirty-six-year-old Scott McClain played in his first major league game in 1998, but he still qualified as a rookie when he joined the Giants on September 3, 2008. He had 362 minor league home runs to his credit, but it still felt pretty sweet when he clubbed his first one in the bigs. McClain and fellow rookies Nate Schierholtz, Pablo Sandoval, and Travis Ishikawa scored all nine Giants runs that day and accounted for all nine RBI.

John Montefusco, 1975

Sandoval, who had not been tabbed as a top prospect, batted .345 in 41 games in 2008. By 2009 he was a fixture in the lineup, proving once again baseball's ability to surprise. Sandoval led the Giants in home runs (25) and RBI (90) and finished second in the National League with a .330 average.

Rookie hazing is alive and well in the Giants clubhouse, with veterans making the stars of tomorrow don embarrassing outfits. During a late-season road trip in 2009, catcher Buster Posey dressed as a barmaid, and pitchers Madison Bumgarner and Dan Runzler were costumed as ketchup and mustard bottles.

The highly touted Posey came up in May 2010 and won Rookie of the Year honors with an outstanding campaign. Not only did the 23 year old hit .305 with 18 homers and 67 RBI, but he shined behind the plate, catching one of baseball's best pitching staffs. In Game Four of the World Series, Posey and Bumgarner, age 21, became the first rookie battery to start a Series game since 1947 and helped the Giants on their way to the championship.

Madison Bumgarner and Buster Posey, 2010 World Series

Buck Ewing, 1889

Roger Bresnahan, 1908

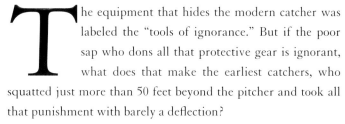

The equipment that hides the modern catcher was labeled the "tools of ignorance." But if the poor sap who dons all that protective gear is ignorant, what does that make the earliest catchers, who squatted just more than 50 feet beyond the pitcher and took all that punishment with barely a deflection?

Buck Ewing, the Giants' first catcher, was one tough customer. The original five-tool player, Ewing is widely considered the greatest ballplayer of the nineteenth century. He batted leadoff, stole bases, caught Hall of Fame pitchers including Mickey Welch and Tim Keefe, gunned down would-be base thieves, and moonlighted at the other eight positions. As the field leader, he often performed the role associated with today's managers; his manager, Jim Mutrie, often sat in the stands. A lifetime

.303 hitter, Ewing played nine years with the Giants and later managed them. He was inducted into the Hall of Fame in 1939.

John McGraw and Roger Bresnahan were a couple of competitive Irishmen who hit it off when they paired up with the old Baltimore Orioles and then came together to the Giants. Bresnahan was a pioneer in catchers' gear, putting padding on his mask, a helmet on his head, and most significantly shin guards on his legs. Opponents mocked him, but the innovations caught on. He was Christy Mathewson's favorite target and a lifetime .279 hitter who peaked with a .350 average in 1902. His plaque is also on display in the Hall of Fame.

McGraw often traded away his favorite players to give them a chance to manage, and he sent Bresnahan to St. Louis after the 1908 season. It helped that McGraw had a worthy successor:

Harry Danning, 1930s

Ernie Lombardi, 1945

John "Chief" Meyers, a Cahuilla Indian from California. Meyers had to overcome a fair amount of discrimination in those days, when baseball wouldn't allow blacks to play, but he held his own catching the likes of Mathewson and Rube Marquard. His three best seasons came for the pennant winners of 1911–1913, when he posted averages of .332, .358, and .312.

Frank "Pancho" Snyder was a career .265 hitter, but for the Giants in 1921 and 1922, he was "Mr. October," batting .364 and .333 in the World Series as the Giants won both times. In 1921 his four hits in Game Three set a record that stood for 61 years.

James "Shanty" Hogan was built like a house—hence the nickname—and was a solid hitter, batting .311 over five years with the Giants from 1928 to 1932. Gus Mancuso caught screwballer Carl Hubbell on the Giants' 1933 champions, and his 840 games behind the plate rank him second in franchise history. A broken finger sidelined Mancuso in 1938, clearing the way for Harry "the Horse" Danning. Danning was an all-star four years in a row (1938–1941), and in a game in 1940, he hit for the cycle;

his home run came when the ball lodged behind the Eddie Grant plaque in the Polo Grounds outfield. Danning was also one of baseball's few Jewish stars, along with Giants first baseman Phil Weintraub. In 1934 during spring training, a Florida hotel refused to admit the Jewish players, until manager Bill Terry threatened to take the entire Giants team elsewhere.

Hall of Famer Ernie Lombardi spent five years at the end of his career with the Giants, still able to wield a ferocious bat, but slower than ever. "He hit the ball so hard, and ran so slow," wrote Bobby Thomson, "that infielders would play him on the outfield grass and still be able to throw him out."

In 1946 Lombardi shared catching duties with Walker Cooper, whom Thomson said "hit the ball harder than anybody I ever played with, and I played with Johnny Mize, Willie Mays, and Henry Aaron." As a full-time starter in 1947, Cooper hit .305 with 35 homers and 122 RBI for the record-setting "Window Breakers" squad. He was the NL's all-star catcher all four years as a Giant.

Wes Westrum, a Giant for 11 seasons, didn't hit much, but he turned in a .999 fielding percentage in 1950—that's one error in 139 games. Tom Haller made two all-star teams in his seven seasons with the Giants in the 1960s, and he is the most common pick for best catcher in the team's San Francisco history. He homered off Whitey Ford in the 1962 World Series.

In 1970 Dick Dietz mounted one of the best single-season performances by a San Francisco catcher, hitting .300 with 22 home runs, 107 RBI, and a home run off Catfish Hunter in the All-Star Game—but 25 passed balls proved his defense was suspect.

They say catchers make good managers. Current Giants' skipper Bruce Bochy probably won't argue with that. Neither would former Giants catcher Bob Brenly, who won a World Series in his first year as the Arizona Diamondbacks' manager. Brenly turned in nine solid years as the Giants' catcher, but his most notable game was September 14, 1986, when he was stationed at third base. On that day, he committed four errors in one inning and allowed four runs to score, but he redeemed himself at the plate, hitting a home run, a two-run single, and finally a tie-breaking,

walk-off home run in the ninth inning to complete his journey from goat to hero. "I went from the outhouse to the penthouse," he said. "If you can come back from something like that, you can come back from anything."

Benito Santiago staged a remarkable comeback with the Giants. The former all-star was nearly through with baseball but arrived in San Francisco in 2001, at age 36. The next year he hit .278, with 27 home runs, and was named MVP of the League Championship Series against the Cardinals.

Slow and steady Bengie Molina—brother of two other major league catchers—led the Giants during their rebuilding years, batting cleanup and guiding a young pitching staff. He was traded to Texas in 2010 and faced the Giants in the World Series.

Buster Posey, the 2010 Rookie of the Year, has the potential to be the Giants' greatest catcher ever. He has shown poise and masterful pitch-calling behind the plate, and cleanup-hitter ability to boot. In his debut season, he hit in 21 straight games, one short of Willie McCovey's Giants rookie record, and his .417 average in July helped keep the team in contention.

Wes Westrum, circa 1948

Bengie Molina, 2009

Buster Posey, 2010

FIRST BASEMEN

First base for the Giants is one of those storied positions in baseball, a position like center field for the Yankees or left field for the Red Sox. Think of it this way: sweet-swinging Will Clark (a six-time all-star) and slick-fielding J. T. Snow (a six-time Gold Glove winner) don't even make the top six at the position in franchise history, taking seats on the pine behind a half dozen Hall of Famers and some of the greatest first sackers in baseball history.

Roger Connor, one of the brightest batting stars of the dead-ball era, held baseball's all-time home run record until Babe Ruth passed him in 1921. Standing 6-foot-3 and weighing 230 pounds, the strapping Connor belted 138 home runs, including the first grand slam in major league history, and he claimed the Giants'

first batting title, hitting .371 in 1885. He was a key cog in the titles of 1888 and 1889.

When the Giants were busy capturing three straight pennants in the 1910s, the first base position was held by a solid player, Fred Merkle, who, as fate dictates, will never be remembered for his hitting or fielding but instead will be remembered for baseball's most infamous base-running blunder (see "Gaffes and Controversies"). Merkle ably manned the position for the Giants from 1910 to 1916, during which time he batted .272 and was a favorite of manager John McGraw.

San Francisco native George "Highpockets" Kelly delivered a Hall of Fame career on McGraw's great teams of the 1920s. At 6-foot-4 and 190 pounds, the power-hitting Kelly brought a new dimension to Little Napoleon's scrappy running attack. He led the league in 1921 with 23 long balls, the biggest of which came in August against the first-place Pittsburgh Pirates. With Kelly facing a 3–0 count, McGraw let him swing away. Kelly blasted the pitch into the railroad yard beyond left field at the Polo Grounds, sparking a Giant sweep and an epic comeback that culminated in a pennant and a World Series win over the Yankees. Kelly also keyed a fine defensive play to record the last out of that Fall Classic.

Roger Connor, 1887

George "Highpockets" Kelly, 1915

Kelly held onto his job even though McGraw brought up a promising replacement from the American Association, and the veteran continued to set records while a young Bill Terry sat on the bench. But by 1925, Kelly was in center field (and was traded a year later) and Terry was at first, a position he occupied for two decades. Memphis Bill became one of the all-time greats, the last National Leaguer to hit .400 (.401 in 1930) and a lifetime .341 hitter (top in franchise history). Just as the Yankees did for his crosstown rival Babe Ruth, the Giants retired Terry's number 3, which hangs from the upper deck at San Francisco's AT&T Park.

While Terry was a Giant from beginning to end, the next truly great player to occupy the position started his career with the Cardinals and ended it with the Yankees. But Johnny Mize—"the Big Cat"—had his best years with the Giants, including an epic 1947 season in which he became the only man ever to slug more than 50 homers (51) while striking out fewer than 50 times (42). His tenure with the Giants would have been even more impressive had he not missed three full seasons to military service in the prime of his career.

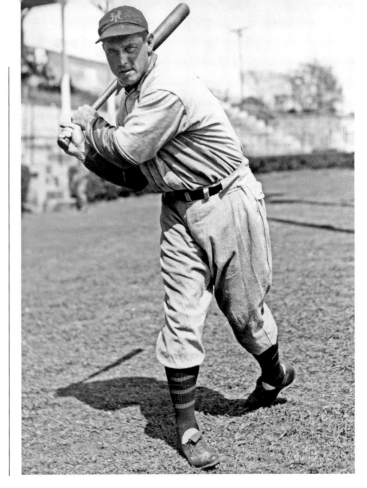

Bill Terry, 1929

Johnny Mize, circa 1947

Orlando Cepeda, early 1960s

Willie McCovey, 1960s

Whitey Lockman moved from the outfield to first base when Willie Mays joined the Giants in 1951, and while he hit a respectable .279 for his career, his old roommate Bobby Thomson praised Lockman as "a clutch and consistent hitter, an outstanding fielder, and, most important, a winner." Lockman's name still gets mentioned in accounts of Thomson's home run, for it was his double that knocked Brooklyn starter Don Newcombe out of the game and put the tying run on base.

When the Giants moved to San Francisco in 1958, Orlando Cepeda burst onto the scene with a home run against Dodger Hall of Famer Don Drysdale in his big league debut. The "Baby Bull"—so named because his father, a major star in Puerto Rico, was known as the Bull—went on to bat .312, with 25 home runs, 96 RBI, and a league-leading 38 doubles, garnering Rookie of the Year honors. The fans were smitten. In nine years with the Giants, Cepeda hit .308 with 226 home runs, a key part of a feared lineup along with Willie Mays and Willie "Stretch" McCovey.

Yes, the Giants were the rare team with two Hall of Famers, in their prime, sharing a position. Just four months younger than Cepeda, McCovey came up to the majors in 1959 and in some ways topped Cepeda's entrance. In his Giants debut, McCovey

went 4-for-4 against Hall of Fame pitcher Robin Roberts, with two triples and two singles—all of which hit the outfield wall at Seals Stadium. "I hit one so hard, it almost bounced all the way back to the infield," he recalled.

Hitting the ball hard was McCovey's hallmark. "McCovey is maybe the scariest batter I ever saw," said writer Roger Angell. "One infielder told me once, 'If there are men on base and Stretch is coming up, I stand a little sideways at third base.'" In his MVP year of 1969—.320 average, 45 home runs, 126 RBI—McCovey was intentionally walked an unheard-of 45 times, including once in the tenth inning with the bases empty. Now that's fear.

Ultimately, the Giants traded Cepeda to give Stretch first base all to himself. And though McCovey was eventually traded as well, he returned to finish his career as a Giant, with 521 career home runs. He remains a fixture at AT&T Park, with a section of the San Francisco Bay called McCovey Cove, where so many Barry Bonds home runs splashed. Giants players vote each year on the winner of the Willie Mac Award, recognizing a teammate for "competitive spirit, ability and leadership," qualities that defined McCovey's long career.

Will Clark, 1992

In 1986 the Giants fielded another outstanding rookie at first. Will "the Thrill" Clark brought a smooth stroke, ever-present eye black, and legendary intensity to the game. Clark homered off Hall of Famer Nolan Ryan in his first at bat and was part of a crew that turned the team into winners again. A lifetime .303 hitter, Clark hit .333 in 1989 and is remembered for many clutch hits, including a single off Chicago's Mitch Williams to send the Giants to the World Series that year.

J. T. Snow joined the Giants in 1997. The first base position is usually known for big boppers, but Snow won the fans over with his glove work—although he did belt a career-best 28 homers in his first year with the Giants. Snow's durability in nine seasons with San Francisco is even more evident in light of the flurry of rookies and veterans who have tried to succeed him.

Aubrey Huff brought stability to the position in 2010. After toiling with losing teams, Huff led the Giants with 26 home runs and 86 RBI, hit .290, and provided veteran leadership and levity in the clubhouse. With 30 games left in the season, Huff donned a rhinestone-studded thong and vowed the team would win 20 of the remaining games—and it did. "The rally thong is going to the Hall of Fame," Huff declared at the victory parade.

J. T. Snow, 2005

SECOND BASEMEN

Danny Richardson, 1887

Larry Doyle, 1912

Second base is known as the keystone position, but for the Giants of the nineteenth century, it was more of a revolving door. Danny Richardson held the job without particularly distinguishing himself in the field or at the plate for three years. Hall of Fame shortstop John Montgomery Ward moved around the horn for the 1893 and 1894 seasons.

Kid Gleason—best known as the unfortunate manager of the 1919 White Sox, but not implicated in the game-fixing scandal—held the post from 1896 to 1900. Gleason, who had been a pitcher before coming to the Giants, batted a career-best .319 with 100 RBI in 1897.

"Laughing Larry" Doyle brought stability to the pivot, but he almost didn't make it. He took the wrong train and was late for his first game in 1907. He then made a mental error during the game,

throwing to first instead of home while the winning run scored. Nevertheless, McGraw stuck with Doyle and wound up with a star. "It's great to be young and a Giant," Doyle declared in 1911. The Giants liked having him as well: he was the National League MVP in 1912, hitting .330 with 10 home runs, 90 RBI, and 36 stolen bases.

Doyle played 13 seasons with the Giants and was team captain from 1908 to 1916. As a Giant, he batted .292 and leads all second basemen with 3,316 putouts and 4,272 assists. He stole home 17 times, including twice in one game, and once finished a 21-inning game with an inside-the-park home run.

When Frankie Frisch joined the Giants in 1919, Doyle was still at second, so the Fordham Flash played third in his first few years, finally becoming the main second sacker in 1922. No matter where Frisch played, McGraw needed his bat in the lineup: in eight years

Frankie Frisch, circa 1923

Eddie Stanky, 1951

with the Giants, Frisch hit .321, posted a .444 slugging percentage, and led the team in stolen bases seven straight years. The Hall of Famer is remembered best as a winner, playing on four pennant winners and three runners-up in his time on the Giants and hitting .363 in the four World Series. (He went on to play on four league champs with the Cardinals, including managing the famed 1934 Gashouse Gang.)

The Giants traded Frisch to the Cardinals for Rogers Hornsby, a swap of Hall of Famers. The Rajah played only one season in New York, but his .361 average, 125 runs, and 106 RBI helped the Giants to a 92-win season, good enough for third place, two games behind pennant-winning Pittsburgh.

The Giants traded for another Cardinals second baseman, Burgess Whitehead, in 1936, and he manned the pivot on back-to-back pennant winners while batting .278 and .286 in 1936 and 1937. After five years with the Giants, World War II interrupted his career.

When Leo Durocher managed the Brooklyn Dodgers in the 1940s, one of his favorite players was Eddie Stanky. "The Lip" and "the Brat" were perfectly paired: fiery, feisty, competitive. So it was natural that, not long after Durocher came to manage the Giants, he traded for Stanky and his double-play partner Alvin Dark to give the team some spunk. Stanky hit .300 with 144 walks in 1950, leading the league with a .460 on-base percentage, and was a key cog on the 1951 pennant team.

Hall of Famer Red Schoendienst came to the Giants midway through the 1956 season and left midway through 1957, batting .301 in his brief stint in New York. Joey Amalfitano held the post for two years, one of his many Giants stints during and after his playing days.

Chuck Hiller hit .276 for the 1962 pennant winners, when he also euphoniously teamed with catcher Tom Haller and pitcher Stu Miller, a trio lampooned in Dodgers fan Danny Kaye's song "The Hiller-Haller-Miller Holler-lujah Twist." Haller and Hiller both homered in the Giants' Game Four win in the World Series that year, with Hiller knocking the first-ever series grand slam by a National Leaguer.

Hal Lanier took over at second in 1964 and shifted over to shortstop when Tito Fuentes arrived on the scene in 1967. "Outside of Bill Mazeroski," said manager Herman Franks,

"I think Tito has the quickest hands in the National League." Fuentes wished Franks had let him use his foot speed more; his six stolen bases in 1966 (when he was used mostly at shortstop) were tops on the Giants, during another in a line of second-place finishes. "I believe we had better teams in those years than the Dodgers, but we didn't play fundamental baseball," he said.

Fuentes played nine years for San Francisco. After he was traded to San Diego in 1975, the Giants were fairly spotty at the position, with a different man taking the job in each of the next seven seasons. One of those men, however, was Bill Madlock—a four-time batting champ as a third baseman on other teams—who played second for the Giants in 1978. Hall of Famer Joe Morgan took the spot for two years toward the end of his career and blasted a memorable Dodger-beating homer in 1982.

Hard-nosed Robby Thompson anchored the position for 11 years, starting in 1986. On the 1989 pennant winners, Thompson led the league in triples, and on the 1993 almost pennant winners, Thompson turned in his best season, hitting .312 with 19 home runs and winning the Gold Glove and Silver Slugger Awards.

Batting ahead of or behind Barry Bonds for his six years with the Giants, Jeff Kent became one of the best-hitting second basemen in history. His 351 career home runs are the new standard for the position, and he won an MVP Award in 2000, when he hit .334 with 33 home runs and 125 RBI. He hit 175 home runs in those six years, and while he famously did not get

Tito Fuentes, early 1970s

Robby Thompson, 1991

Jeff Kent, 2002

along with Bonds—the two even fought in the dugout during a game—he thrived with the big guy hitting near him.

Since Kent's departure, the Giants have tried a number of second basemen. Veteran Ray Durham did most of the work from 2003 to 2008, and in 2006 he chipped in with a .293 average, 26 homers, and 93 RBI. He was traded for a couple of prospects in July 2008, handing over the second base job to rookies Eugenio Velez and Emmanuel Burris.

Exasperated that no one seemed able to win the keystone job, general manager Brian Sabean traded for former batting champ and all-star Freddy Sanchez in July 2009. Sanchez soon won admirers with his fancy glove work and steady batsmanship. After hitting .292 during the regular season, he drew notice with his outstanding play in the 2010 World Series, leaping to spear line drives and doubling in his first three at-bats.

Ray Durham, 2006

SHORTSTOPS

John Montgomery "Monte" Ward could play any position. As a pitcher, mostly with the Providence Grays before the Giants were established, he had a 2.10 ERA over seven seasons and once won 47 games. But his arm wore out, and he spent the bulk of his 17-year career as a shortstop. If the Gothams' first-ever game was any indication, he was needed: shortstop Dasher Troy committed five errors as the Giants lost to the Boston Beaneaters 7–5.

Ward goes down in the history books for organizing a players' union as well as a players' league that broke away from the National League, but his leadership ability off the field was matched by his talents on it. In 1887 Ward hit .338 and led the league with a .919 fielding percentage and 111 stolen bases. (That record does not stand up to modern rules; the tally includes extra bases he took on hits or outs.)

George Davis was primarily a third baseman when he came to the Giants in 1893, but he moved to short full-time in 1897, and his Hall of Fame plaque refers to him as "a shortstop of shining prominence." He never hit below .300 in his 10 years in New York, and he topped .350 three times. Davis led the league in RBI with 136 in 1897, and he served as player-manager for the 1898, 1900, and 1901 Giants. His 33-game hitting streak in 1893 was a record at the time.

When John McGraw traded for "Bad Bill" Dahlen in 1904, he chose a player in his own image. "Now I have the man I've

John Montgomery Ward, Allen & Ginter tobacco card, 1887

Art Fletcher, 1917

wanted ever since I've had charge of this team," McGraw said of the pugnacious veteran. Dahlen was happy to leave the Dodgers. "It has always been my ambition to play in New York City," he said. "Brooklyn is all right, but if you're not with the Giants, you might as well be in Albany." (Dahlen later returned to manage the Dodgers for four years.) With the 1904 pennant-winning Giants, Dahlen drove in a league-high 80 runs.

Al Bridwell, who played shortstop for the Giants from 1908 to 1911, lives on mostly as a footnote: it was his hit that led to the famous "Merkle Boner" in the 1908 game against the Cubs. Bridwell's successor at shortstop, Art Fletcher, played 12 years for the Giants, playing on four pennant winners and contributing a .275 average over that span.

Stuck in second place, the Giants traded Fletcher, pitcher Bill Hubbell, and $100,000 for Dave "Beauty" Bancroft in 1920. Bancroft hit a combined .316 from 1921 to 1923 as part of a Hall of Fame infield (with Frankie Frisch and George Kelly) that won the pennant each year and two World Series. In 1923 he came down with pneumonia and missed more than 40 games. His replacement, Travis Jackson, played well enough that season that John McGraw traded Bancroft to the Braves. Jackson went on to a 15-year Hall of Fame career with the Giants, playing more games at shortstop for the franchise than anyone else. In 1930 he was part of the best-hitting infield in history, batting .339 while first baseman Bill Terry hit .401, third baseman Freddie Lindstrom hit .379, and second baseman Hughie Critz batted .265—a composite .349 average. A lifetime .291 hitter, Jackson was known for his great range and rifle arm at short.

When Terry became the manager, he identified the missing ingredient in getting the Giants back to the World Series and traded four players and cash to the Phillies for feisty shortstop Dick Bartell. While "Rowdy Richard" hit only .262 in 1935, he batted .298 and .306 the next two years, and Terry, second baseman Burgess Whitehead, and Bartell formed a tight infield for back-to-back pennant winners.

A pair of native New Yorkers—Billy Jurges and Buddy Kerr—held the post through the 1940s. Each turned in some all-star seasons and some fine glove work, but it was the 1949 trade for shortstop Alvin Dark (and second baseman Eddie Stanky) that many say brought the Giants back to the postseason. Dark hit .303 in the pennant year of 1951 and led the league with 41 doubles. He posted a combined .415 average in the World Series of 1951 and 1954. Dark later returned to the Giants as manager and led the team to the 1962 series.

Travis Jackson, circa 1922

Alvin Dark, 1952

Jose Pagan, 1962

Royce Clayton, 1994

Rich Aurilia, 2007

Shortstop Daryl Spencer hit the first home run on the West Coast in 1958. He had hit 20 home runs in 1953, a record for rookie shortstops that stood for 50 years, but then Leo Durocher changed his swing. "I was a dead pull hitter, and he wanted me to hit to right field," Spencer said. "I think back a lot to 1953. What if Durocher left me alone? I would have hit 35 home runs."

On a team of sluggers, Jose Pagan was a 5-foot-9 shortstop who led the league in fielding in 1962. He was "the silent anchor of our infield," according to manager Dark. Pagan even homered in the World Series that year. He manned the position until getting traded for fellow shortstop Dick Schofield early in the 1965 season.

When Chris Speier became the shortstop in 1971, the team filled a long-standing hole—and returned to the postseason. A .246 lifetime hitter, Speier batted .357 and hit a home run in the 1971 NLCS. Throughout the early 1970s, Speier formed a slick double-play combo with Tito Fuentes. He once recalled that manager Charlie Fox had told him to "take charge of the infield, because he said Willie McCovey didn't say too much and Tito Fuentes talked too much and you couldn't understand him. But it was something to work with Tito. He was quick and flashy and we really jelled together." Speier, a three-time all-star, was a rock at short until 1977, when he was traded for shortstop Tim Foli. Speier returned to San Francisco as a free agent in 1987 to finish out his career before retiring in 1989.

Johnnie LeMaster came in after Foli's one-year stay and was another in a long line of good-fielding, weak-hitting Giant shortstops. Although he hit an inside-the-park home run in his first big league at bat in 1975, he hit only 22 for his career, and his average never topped .253. The fans at Candlestick were on him so much that he once came to the park wearing a shirt with "Boo" printed on the back.

Neither was Jose Uribe in the game for his bat, although he hit .291 for the 1987 division champs. His glove was enough to keep him in the lineup for seven years. The arrival of first-round draft pick Royce Clayton in 1992 pushed Uribe out, and then the story takes a familiar turn: Clayton hit .282 for the 1993 team that won 103 games, but the hits gradually became fewer and farther between, and he was traded away after the 1995 season.

But again the Giants had a kid waiting in the wings, and this one could swing a stick. Brooklyn-born Rich Aurilia hit .277 over his first eight seasons and even became something of a slugger. In 2001 he hit .324, with 37 home runs and 97 RBI, and led the league with 206 hits. Although he left as a free agent in 2004, Aurilia returned in 2007 as a steady utility infielder.

In 2005 the Giants signed one of the greatest shortstops of all, Omar Vizquel. As he barehanded balls and fielded with dexterity never seen before, Vizquel hit .271 and .295 and won Gold Gloves in his first two seasons in San Francisco. The Giants kept him as he turned 40, and although his batting fell off, his defense continued to support the young pitchers coming up. Vizquel's colorful wardrobe, including his orange shoes, and his love of art and music made him a perfect fit in San Francisco.

With Vizquel's departure, many fans thought the Giants would go with the youth movement and promote a minor leaguer to the position. Instead, they surprised many in 2009 by signing 14-year veteran Edgar Renteria. After battling injuries in 2010, Renteria showed one final flash of his old form, and it came at the right time. His winning home run in Game Five and .412 series average helped him bring home the World Series MVP trophy.

Omar Vizquel, 2008

Art Devlin, 1911

THIRD BASEMEN

The Giants of the nineteenth century never got much offense out of their third basemen until George Stacey Davis came over from the old Cleveland Spiders and started hitting the tar out of what is now known as a dead ball. Davis hit .355 and .352 in his first two years with the Giants (1893 and 1894) and averaged more than 100 RBI over his first four seasons in New York. By 1897 he had moved to shortstop, on his way to a Hall of Fame career.

Writer Frank Graham, in his mid-century book on the Giants, declared Art Devlin "the greatest third baseman ever to wear a Giant uniform." Devlin's expert handling of the hot corner anchored the Giants' infield from 1904 to 1911. His greatest contribution to the team may have come after his playing career, however, when he was the baseball coach at Fordham University and told manager John McGraw to send someone up to scout a player. "This is a real ball player, Mac," Devlin said. And that's how the Giants got Frankie Frisch.

Freddie Lindstrom did not have Devlin's artistry in the field, but Devlin never showed Lindstrom's prowess at the plate, and that's why Lindstrom is in the Hall of Fame and Devlin isn't. Lindstrom's most famous moment in the field ended the 1924 World Series, when—with the score tied in the bottom of the twelfth—he prepared to field an inning-ending double play. Instead, the ball hit a rock, hopped over his head,

Freddie Lindstrom, late 1920s

and the Senators' winning run scored from second. Six weeks shy of his nineteenth birthday, he was the youngest player ever to appear in the World Series. Four years later, when he hit .358, led the league with 231 hits, and drove in 107 runs, Lindstrom was runner-up for the league MVP in 1928. He batted .379 in 1930, forming a devastating combo with first baseman Bill Terry, who hit .401.

After a four-year run by Johnny Vergez, from 1931 to 1934, the hot corner became a hot seat for the Giants. Over the next 15 years, a wide variety of players were tried at the position, from shortstops Travis Jackson and Dick Bartell to second basemen Burgess Whitehead and Bill Rigney to outfielder Mel Ott, who wielded a mighty bat but was less than masterful in the field.

Manager Ott gave utility man Sid Gordon a steady job at third in 1948, and Gordon, one of New York's few legitimate Jewish stars, responded with a .299 average, 30 home runs, and 107 RBI. The next year he hit .284, with 26 homers and 90 RBI, for Leo Durocher, who then shipped him to the Boston Braves in the trade that brought Alvin Dark and Eddie Stanky to New York.

Hank Thompson—the Giants' first black player along with Monte Irvin—hit .289 with 20 homers and 90 RBI while playing third base in 1950. He held the position for the next

Sid Gordon, circa 1949

Hank Thompson, 1957

Jim Davenport, 1962 World Series

five years, although when he was injured in 1951, Bobby Thomson came in to play third, making room for the new centerfielder Willie Mays. Hank Thompson batted a career-best .302 in 1953 and then contributed 26 homers and 86 RBI to the 1954 pennant team.

Among the fine newcomers joining the Giants in San Francisco was third baseman Jim Davenport, whom Alvin Dark called "the greatest third baseman I ever saw." Davenport's glove work was a key ingredient for the 1962 NL champs, and he earned an all-star selection and a Gold Glove Award that year. Davenport spent his entire 13-year playing career with the Giants and worked for the team for 45 of his 51 years in baseball, even managing in 1985 (before getting fired with the team on its way to 100 losses). Nobody has played more games for the Giants at the hot corner than Davenport.

Jim Ray Hart took over in 1964, blasting 31 home runs and hitting .286. He actually broke in a year earlier but had one of those "welcome to the big leagues" moments in his second game, when Bob Gibson broke his shoulder blade with a fastball. Hart made it back to the lineup in August, and four days later the Cardinals' Curt Simmons beaned him, sending him to the hospital. Over the next five years, Hart averaged .285, 28 homers, and 89 RBI, but his fielding suffered later in his career and Davenport won the job back.

Darrell Evans hit 40 homers before coming to the Giants in 1976, and he hit 40 after leaving in 1983, but Candlestick winds kept many of his long flies from leaving the park. He did hit 30 in 1983, when he batted .277 and made the all-star team. His 1,605 career walks are good for twelfth on baseball's all-time list.

On "turn back the clock" days, Matt Williams always looked right at home in a nineteenth-century uniform. Matty was one of the best in the bigs at third base during his years with the Giants, and the fans hated to see him go. He became the regular third baseman in 1990, breaking out with 33 homers, a league-leading 122 RBI, and a .277 average. The next year he won the first of his three Gold Gloves with the Giants. In his 10 years in San Francisco, Williams hit 247 home runs, ranking him fifth on the all-time franchise list behind Bonds, Mays, McCovey, and Ott. Pretty good company.

Bill Mueller was a rookie in Williams' final season with the Giants, and the next year he became the starter. Another steady fan favorite, Mueller was never flashy and consistently hit in the neighborhood of .290. It was no surprise to Giants fans when he won a batting title as the number-nine hitter on the 2003 Red Sox.

Matt Williams, 1990

Pablo Sandoval, 2009

David Bell spent one season with the Giants, 2002, and he followed up an unspectacular regular season by hitting .412 in the NLCS and .304 in the World Series, contributing a homer in each round. Pedro Feliz was Bell's backup on the pennant winners, and a year later he shared the post with Edgardo Alfonzo. After moving around between first, third, and the outfield, Feliz took hold of the third base job in 2006. He never quite lived up to his potential at the plate in his eight years with the Giants, always hitting about .250 and 20 home runs in each season.

As Bruce Bochy scrambled to fill his lineup card in 2008, 21-year-old Pablo Sandoval came along as something of a revelation, starting the year at single-A San Jose and rising to the big league club by mid-August. Beefy and good natured, Sandoval just kept hitting. He hit .345 and followed that with a .330 average in 2009—second best in the National League. He also chipped in 44 doubles and 25 home runs, while making improbably acrobatic plays in the field. Sandoval slumped to .268 and 13 home runs in 2010, but his devoted fans kept wearing their panda hats in honor of the "Kung Fu Panda" at the hot corner.

OUTFIELDERS

The huge outfields at the Polo Grounds and AT&T Park, and the windy ones at Candlestick, have been patrolled by some of the greatest ever, including record-setting sluggers Mel Ott, Willie Mays, and Barry Bonds.

It was in a different Polo Grounds, where polo actually had been played, that the first Giants roamed the field. The championship squads of 1888 and 1889 had an odd pair of outfield stars: "Orator Jim" O'Rourke, given to lengthy rhetoric, and "Silent Mike" Tiernan. O'Rourke, who registered the first hit in National League history as a member of the Boston Red Stockings in 1876, joined the Giants in 1885 on his way to a .310 lifetime average and the Hall of Fame.

O'Rourke achieved some unusual distinctions. In 1904—when he was 54 and 11 years into his retirement—John McGraw put him in the lineup as catcher, and he became the oldest person to play a full game. (He went one for four and scored a run.) He later served as president of the Connecticut League while also working as a player-manager of a team in that league. In one game, he cursed out an umpire—and then announced that, in his capacity as president, he was fining himself for undiplomatic behavior.

Tiernan played 13 seasons with the Giants (1887–1899), and he remains the all-time franchise leader in triples with 162 and in steals with 428 (although quite a few of those would not count under today's rules). He ranks among the top 10 in most offensive

Jim O'Rourke, 1888

George Burns, 1922

Ross Youngs, circa 1918

Irish Meusel, 1923

categories, and he scored six runs in the Giants' epic 29–1 win over Philadelphia in 1887.

Leading off and playing left field for manager John McGraw from 1913 to 1921 was another quiet but steady performer, "Silent George" Burns, whom McGraw called "one of the most valuable ball players that ever wore the uniform of the Giants." Burns led the league in runs five times and stolen bases twice. He was one of the first players to wear sunglasses and a long-billed cap; his teammates called him the greatest "sunfielder" in the game. Burns handled left field with such expertise that the bleachers there became known as Burnsville.

McGraw kept photos of two players in his office at the Polo Grounds: Christy Mathewson and right fielder Ross "Pep" Youngs. Youngs was one of his favorites. He starred

for the Giants during 10 glorious seasons, posting a lifetime average of .322 and falling below .300 only once (in 1925), when he was ill. That illness proved to be serious, what was then called Bright's disease and is now the kidney disorder known as acute nephritis. It took Youngs' life in 1927, at age 30. He was inducted into the Hall of Fame in 1972.

Youngs' steadiest outfield mate was Emil "Irish" Meusel, who hit .314 in his six years with the Giants but was overshadowed by his brother Bob Meusel, whose Yankees won six pennants and four World Series. The Giants in Youngs' tenure had a rotating cast of noteworthy center fielders, including Casey Stengel, Hack Wilson, and Edd Roush—Hall of Famers all—but never at the right time in their careers and for only a year at a time.

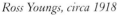

Mel Ott, circa 1936

People can debate whether Mays was the greatest ever to play the game, but if he wasn't, there aren't too many others ahead of him on that list. Everyone who saw or played with the "Say Hey Kid" has a story of his remarkable, ethereal ability. "The average person in the stands didn't recognize what he did. He was just that good," said Willie McCovey, a Hall of Famer in his own right who followed Mays in the lineup for so many years. "He made catches that he took for granted, and I see guys making catches like that now that they write about for a week."

"Boy, he could do everything," Daryl Spencer said, thinking to how Mays would never even need to hit a cut-off man—his throws sailed straight to their target, even if it was home plate. Jim Davenport said, "It was unbelievable to see what he could do on the field."

One of the few true five-tool players, Mays held onto center field for the Giants from 1951 to 1971, except for two early years (most of 1952 and all of 1953) lost to the army. He won two MVP awards (1954 and 1965) and 12 straight Gold Gloves. In his 23-year career, he batted .302, hit 660 home runs, knocked 3,283 hits, drove in 1,903 runs, and stole 336 bases. In the words of his first manager, Leo Durocher, "Joe Louis, Jascha Heifetz, Sammy Davis, and Nashua rolled into one."

Mays had many companions in his Giant run. When Thomson shifted over to left field (and third base), he continued to produce, driving in more than 100 runs in three straight years. Don Mueller—"Mandrake the Magician"—covered right field from 1950 to 1957 and batted .297 during that span. He hit .342 in 1954 but lost to Mays' .345 mark. Because of baseball's color barrier, Monte Irvin was 30 years old by the time he reached the majors, but he still turned in several solid years en route to the Hall of Fame. In 1951 he had a .312 average, 24 homers, and a league-leading 121 RBI. Thomson said that without Irvin, the Giants never would have reached that playoff with the Dodgers. Irvin then batted .458 in a losing effort against the Yankees in the World Series.

In San Francisco, the Alou brothers arrived. Felipe, the oldest, landed first in 1958. Matty came up two years later, and Jesus, the baby, in 1963. Felipe had the best single season among them in 1962, when he hit .316 with 25 homers and 98 RBI. Once in 1963 they all batted in the same half inning but did not manage a hit. Twice that season they filled the outfield together. Combined, the Alou brothers totaled 5,094 hits in their career, more than any other brother combo in history. Keeping it all in the family, Felipe returned to manage the Giants from 2003 to 2006, and his son Moises starred in the outfield for two of those years.

It seems funny to call Mel Ott—who stood only 5-foot-9—a Giant. But opponents were not amused. They walked him almost as if he had Eddie Gaedel's strike zone. Ott led the league in bases on balls six times, and he walked 80 or more times for 14 straight seasons. A look at Ott's other numbers explains why pitchers opted so often to give him a free pass: he packed a lot of power in that small frame, leading the league in homers six times and averaging 28 homers and 101 RBI per year from 1928 to 1945. A 12-time all-star, Ott was a Giant for his entire career and later managed the team.

Ott manned right field, while Jo-Jo Moore was his most common mate in left field. From 1932 to 1941, Moore batted .298 and made six all-star teams. Center field was again the spot the Giants couldn't quite fill with a reliable presence. Bobby Thomson seemed the most likely candidate when he joined the team in 1947, and he batted .275 and averaged 24 homers through his first four full seasons. And then along came Willie Mays.

Willie Mays, 1954 World Series

Bobby Bonds, early 1970s

Jack Clark, 1983

Like folksingers anointed the next Bob Dylan and thereby doomed to failure, Bobby Bonds was called the next Willie Mays when he signed with the Giants in 1964. He did reach some heights during his seven years with the team, including winning three Gold Gloves and becoming only the second man (after Mays) to hit 30 homers and steal 30 bases in the same season, something he went on to do five times. He, his close friend Mays, his son Barry, and four others are the only members of the 300–300 club. But while he was a formidable combination of speed and power, Bonds also set strikeout records, and he wound up playing for eight teams in his career while batting .268 lifetime. Teammate Tito Fuentes said he was a better player than his son, but "he didn't work at his game. It was too easy for him."

In the early 1970s, Bonds teamed with Gary Matthews and Garry Maddox in the Giants outfield. "I would think in that era we were the fastest outfield in baseball," Matthews said.

Jack "the Ripper" Clark was a fearsome hitter and a famously surly presence on the Giants from 1977 to 1984. In the team's 1982

run, which fell just short of the playoffs, he hit .274 with 27 homers and 103 RBI. Colorful characters dotted the Candlestick greenery in the 1980s, and some could actually hit—Chili Davis, Candy Maldonado, Jeffrey Leonard, and Dan Gladden among them. The 1989 NL champs featured league MVP Kevin Mitchell (.291, 47 homers, 125 RBI) and leadoff sparkplug Brett Butler (.283, 31 steals).

And then came Barry. Barry Bonds was known in the Giants clubhouse since he was a kid following his dad around. By the time he joined the Giants in 1993, he had already won two MVP awards with the Pirates, and many think his abrasive personality robbed him of a third in 1991. His first year with the Giants brought tremendous numbers and another MVP trophy, as he led the league with 46 homers, 123 RBI, a .458 on-base percentage, and a .677 slugging percentage. Astonishingly, none of those would turn out to be career highs.

Bonds was good throughout the 1990s, but when he turned 35 in 2000, his game reached a level achieved by only

Barry Bonds, August 7, 2007

a handful of players ever. He won four straight MVP awards (he lost in 2000 to teammate Jeff Kent in a close vote). In 2001 he hit 73 home runs, playing in only 153 games. The next year, he won his first batting title with a .370 average. By 2004 he rarely saw a good pitch to hit, walking 232 times—an astounding 120 of those intentional, both all-time records—and he still managed to lead the league with a .362 average while clubbing 45 home runs. Over the five seasons from 2000 to 2004, Bonds averaged 51 homers, 108 RBI, 123 runs, and 174 walks, while batting .339, slugging .781, and reaching base at a .535 clip.

Many believe that Bonds' association with baseball's steroids scandals will forever taint his records. Clothing designer Marc Ecko bought his 756th home run ball for $750,000, branded it with an asterisk, and sent it to Cooperstown, where it is on display in the Baseball Hall of Fame. The steroid controversy may keep Bonds out of the Hall. He testified that if he did use steroids, he didn't know it, and he has fought a lengthy court battle against perjury charges for the claim. The Giants didn't sign him after the 2007 season, and he has not played since.

The Giants had two strategies for Bonds' outfield partners: good gloves such as Darren Lewis, Darryl Hamilton, and Jose Cruz Jr., and big boppers such as Ellis Burks and Reggie Sanders.

Adres Torres, 2010

Since letting Bonds go, the Giants have combined veterans like Randy Winn (2005–2009) and Aaron Rowand with youngsters like Nate Schierholtz. In 2010, speedy journeyman Andres Torres discovered a hitting stroke and took over center field, providing the Giants with the leadoff man they lacked for years. Pat Burrell and Cody Ross, waived by their former teams, arrived in mid-season to give the Giants a championship outfield.

HOME RUN HEROES

The Giants have played in some of the most cavernous parks in baseball, yet they've had many of the game's greatest sluggers as well.

In their first year in the National League, 1883, catcher Buck Ewing led the league with 10 home runs. This was the dead-ball era, when home runs were few. Softer than today's balls to begin with, one ball was usually used for an entire game, and it became a tattered sphere that pitchers routinely doctored. It was hard to hit for any distance, particularly in parks that had center field fences extending more than 500 feet from home plate.

The big first baseman on the 1883 team, Roger Connor, hit only one home run that year. But by the time he retired in 1897, Connor was the all-time home run king, with a whopping 138. His record stood until 1921, when Babe Ruth passed him en route to his record 714.

Manager John McGraw didn't believe in the home run and instead favored "inside baseball." He once fined Red Murray for hitting a game-winning home run when McGraw had ordered him to bunt. By the time Ruth came around, however, McGraw had to make concessions, and he brought up another big guy, George Kelly.

Kelly's 6-foot-4 stature earned him the nicknamed Highpockets. A native San Franciscan, Kelly led the league with 23 home runs for the 1921 champions, the first time a Giants player reached 20 in a season.

You didn't have to be big to hit home runs, which Mel Ott amply proved. Only 5-foot-9 and 170 pounds, Ott deployed a high leg kick that put tremendous power into his swings. McGraw

Roger Connor, 1888

Mel Ott, 1935

Willie Mays, 1967

Barry Bonds, 2001

didn't want any minor league manager messing with that swing, so he brought Ott up to the big leagues at age 17. Ott took advantage of the Polo Grounds' 257-foot right field porch and led the league in homers six times. He led the Giants in home runs for 18 straight years; no one has ever done that on any team. He became the first National Leaguer to hit 500, finishing at 511. He passed Rogers Hornsby in 1937 to become the NL career record holder, and he held the top spot until another Giant, Willie Mays, passed him in 1966.

Ott was done hitting home runs by 1947, but he managed the club known as the Window Breakers. The Giants that year set a team record with 221 home runs, led by Johnny Mize's 51. With Willard Marshall (36), Walker Cooper (35), and Bobby Thomson (29), the Giants had four of the league's top five sluggers.

Many believe Mays might have passed Babe Ruth if he hadn't lost almost two full years in his prime to military service during the Korean War. In his first year back, 1954, he hit 41 home runs and was the league MVP; in 1955 he belted a league-high 51. Mays finished his career with 660 homers (all but 14 of them for the Giants).

For a few years, Mays anchored what was the most feared batting order in baseball, hitting ahead of Willie McCovey and Orlando Cepeda. In 1963 alone, the trio combined for 168 home runs. Cepeda hit 226 homers in just over seven seasons with the team. McCovey went on to knock 521 career home runs, 469 of

them for the Giants, and led the National League three times in an era that featured the likes of Mays, Hank Aaron, and Ernie Banks, among other formidable sluggers.

After McCovey led the senior circuit with 45 homers in 1969, no Giants player won a home run crown until Kevin Mitchell blasted 47 in his MVP year of 1989. The next year, Mitchell and teammate Matt Williams finished third and fourth in the league with 35 and 33 homers, respectively. In 1994 Williams had 43 home runs after just 115 games, on pace to break Roger Maris' single-season record of 61, when the baseball players went on strike.

Although great things were expected when Bobby Bonds came up with the Giants in 1968, and he did prove to be a slugging and base-stealing threat, it was his child who shattered every home run record in baseball. Barry Bonds—Bobby's son and Mays' godson—is featured on many plaques lining McCovey Cove, where so many of his splash hits landed.

Bonds holds the mark for most home runs in a season, with 73 in 2001, and in 2007 he passed Aaron as the all-time home run king before finishing his career with 762. When, in 2004, he hit career home run number 660 to tie Mays on the all-time list, Bonds declared, "It just kind of binded us all together, my dad and Willie and myself. . . . Everybody said my dad was the next Willie Mays. They just got the name wrong, from Bobby to Barry."

RIGHT-HANDED PITCHERS

In the dead-ball era, the ball wasn't the only thing that was expected to last an entire game. The starting pitcher was as well. The statistics for some of the Giants' early aces boggle the mind of a modern fan accustomed to pitch counts and "quality starts."

"Smiling Mickey" Welch stood only 5-foot-8 and was just 23 years old during the Gothams' maiden season, but he was already a three-year veteran, with 69 wins to his credit, and a workhorse ready to go. He hurled 426 innings and had a 25–23 record that year, but it was just the beginning. The next three years he won 39, 44, and 33 games, topping 490 innings each year. Welch never led the league in innings pitched, however; his 557 innings in 1884 was only fourth most in the league, as Charley "Old Hoss" Radbourn threw a league-high 678.

Welch had 307 wins and a 2.71 ERA in his 13-year career, and he was a fan favorite for the poems he'd effortlessly toss off, most famously about his love of beer. When he was reunited with his old Troy teammate "Sir Timothy" Keefe in 1885, the Giants were almost unstoppable. In the era of a two-man rotation, boasting a tandem of Hall of Famers led the team to titles in 1888 and 1889. In 1888 Keefe won 19 straight games—still a record, tied only by Giants Rube Marquard and Carl Hubbell—and won pitching's triple crown, going 35–12 with a 1.74 ERA and 335 strikeouts.

In 1890 Keefe joined many teammates in jumping to the new Players League, but Welch stayed with the Giants, where he was joined by 19-year-old Amos Rusie. As a rookie, Rusie led the league in walks (289, a record that still stands), strikeouts, wild pitches, and losses. But he also won 29 games, and the next four

Mickey Welch, 1888

Amos Rusie, 1890s

Christy Mathewson, 1912

Joe McGinnity, 1908

years he topped 30 wins every time. In 1891 he became the youngest pitcher ever to throw a no-hitter. Rusie left the team in 1896 in a spat over wages with wacky owner Andrew Freedman, but by then he was such a drawing card that the other owners chipped in to bring him back. The "Hoosier Thunderbolt" was also a terror on the field; one of his beanballs left Hall of Famer Hughie Jennings in a coma for four days, and Rusie's heat from the mound helped convince the league to move the pitchers' mound back from 50 feet to home plate to its present-day 60 feet, 6 inches.

Rusie was finally traded away, and in return the Giants got the greatest of them all, the best pitcher ever to grace their mound: Christy Mathewson. With his trademark fadeaway (a variation on a screwball), Mathewson won 373 games, the most in National League history and third most of all time; his lifetime ERA of 2.13 is eighth best of all time. No one has equaled his record of 12 straight 20-win seasons, a stretch that included four seasons with 30 or more wins. He twice won the pitching triple crown: in 1905,

with 31 wins, a 1.28 ERA, and 206 strikeouts; and in 1908, when he went 37–11 with a 1.43 ERA and 259 strikeouts. His catcher, Chief Meyers, said, "He had perfect control. Really, almost perfect." In 1913 he had a stretch of 68 straight innings without issuing a walk, and he finished the year with 21 walks in 306 innings.

Tall, handsome, and college educated, the fan favorite formed an unlikely partnership with short, combative Muggsy McGraw, and they dominated baseball in the early years of the last century. Mathewson was never thrown out of a game. He was among the first class of inductees into baseball's Hall of Fame in 1936.

Matty joined a rotation that already included Hall of Famer "Iron Man" Joe McGinnity. McGinnity worked in his father-in-law's iron mill, but he earned the nickname as well for his iron arm on the mound. He pitched 314 complete games in his 10-year career, and he thrice pitched complete games to win both ends of a double-header. He and Mathewson were a formidable pair of aces, each topping 30 wins in 1903 and 1904.

Larry Jansen, 1950s

Juan Marichal, circa 1965

The Giants have sent other notable right-handers to the mound over the years. Jeff Tesreau won 115 games in a little more than six seasons before breaking ties with McGraw and quitting the Giants in 1918 to coach at Dartmouth College. Lefty Carl Hubbell teamed with righty "Fat Freddie" Fitzsimmons, who was 170–114 (.599) from 1925 to 1937, and with "Prince Hal" Schumacher, who went 158–121 (.566) from 1931 to 1946.

As a 26-year-old rookie in 1946, Larry Jansen went 21–5, launching a five-year stretch in which he won 96 games. Sal Maglie joined in 1950 and had his own five-year run totaling 81 wins. With Jim Hearn, the three righties combined for 63 of the Giants' 98 wins in the glorious 1951 season. That year, Maglie—known as the Barber for both his perpetual five o'clock shadow and his willingness to give batters a close shave—had a bet with Jansen to see who could win more games. As the Giants headed into the last of their three-game playoff with the Dodgers, Maglie held the lead, 23 to 22, and was starting that game. But he left trailing 4–1, and Jansen came in and kept the Dodgers from scoring in the ninth. In the bottom half, the impossible happened: Bobby Thomson homered, the Giants won, and Jansen tied Maglie for the league lead with 23 wins.

Jack Sanford won 89 games in his six-plus Giant seasons, but it was the 1962 season that lives in San Francisco memory. Sanford was the ace on that pennant-winning staff, with a record of 24–7 (.774) and a 3.43 ERA. That was also the coming-out season for Juan Marichal, who was 18–11 with a 3.36 ERA. In 1963 "the Dominican Dandy" went 25–8, the start of a run of six 20-win seasons in seven years, each time striking out more than 200 batters and his ERA never rising above 2.50—a stretch of dominance that put him into the Hall of Fame. His high leg kick is immortalized in a statue outside AT&T Park, the only Giants pitcher so honored.

Gaylord Perry, 1966

Rick Reuschel, 1990

Gaylord Perry was an up-and-coming pitcher whose career foundered until the Giants picked up little-remembered reliever Bob Shaw in 1964. Shaw had something in his repertoire that he was happy to teach Perry: a spitball. Perry once claimed—but later retracted, as he now denies throwing the greaser—that the spitter and a hard slider, which Larry Jansen taught him, helped turned his career around. Perry was the winning pitcher in the 1966 All-Star Game, and he was 20–2 at one point in the season, ultimately finishing 21–8 with a 2.99 ERA.

"I reckon I tried everything on the old apple, but salt and pepper and chocolate sauce topping," Perry once wrote. Rival manager Gene Mauch once suggested that Perry's Hall of Fame plaque have "a tube of KY jelly attached."

Giants righties have had their moments. Consider John "Count" Montefusco's 1974 debut. He was brought into a game and had to work out of a bases-loaded, no-out jam, which he did—and then homered in his first at bat to help win his first game. Although he won 31 games in his first two full seasons, including a no-hitter in 1976, he never lived up to his potential or his own brash predictions for greatness.

Rick Reuschel, "Big Daddy," arrived in 1987 on a staff that boasted Mike Krukow (20–9 in 1986) and helped provide the boost to win the division. Over the next two years, the 6-foot-3, 235-pound Reuschel posted marks of 19–11 and 17–8, anchoring the pennant-winning staff of 1989. Scott Garrelts, who pitched 10 years with the Giants, picked that year to shine: he was 14–5 and led the league in winning percentage (.737) and ERA (2.28).

In the amazing 1993 season, which saw new owners, new manager Dusty Baker, and 103 wins, but no postseason play, two righties had career years: Bill Swift went 21–8 with a 2.82 ERA, and John Burkett went 22–7 with a 3.65 ERA.

After several lean years, an effort to build a staff paid off in 2002 with another pennant. Russ Ortiz led the way in victories, with records of 18–9 in 1999 and 17–9 in 2001. Livan Hernandez came over from Florida and won 45 games in three-plus seasons. And a trade for Pittsburgh power pitcher Jason Schmidt turned the 2002 season around, as he wrapped up the year 7–1. Schmidt was a Cy Young contender in 2003 (17–5, 2.34) and 2004 (18–7, 3.20).

Matt Cain has been an astounding hard-luck story, pitching well but rarely getting run support. His respectable ERA of 3.45 in his first six seasons makes it hard to swallow his 57–62 record. He dominated in the 2010 postseason, throwing 21⅓ innings without surrendering an earned run.

Baby-faced Tim Lincecum joined Cain in the rotation in 2007, and the next year, his first full season, Lincecum captured the Giants' first Cy Young Award since Mike McCormick in 1967. Lincecum went 18–5 with a 2.62 ERA and a league-leading 265 strikeouts. The slightly built pitcher with the unusual motion did it again in 2009, going 15–7 with a 2.48 ERA, to become the first pitcher ever to win back-to-back Cy Youngs in his first two full seasons. He was 16–10 in 2010 and led the league in strikeouts for the third straight year, with 231. The long-haired "Freak"—or "Franchise"—was an ace in the playoffs, winning four games, including the World Series clincher.

Matt Cain, 2008

Tim Lincecum, 2009

LEFT-HANDED PITCHERS

The term *southpaw* is believed to have originated in baseball. Ballparks are oriented so that batters face east, rather than have to squint into afternoon sunlight. That means a left-handed pitcher's arm points south when he's facing the batter.

The relative rarity of left-handers in the general population probably accounts for how few pitched in baseball's early days. But when the Giants won their first championship in 1888, it was thanks in part to journeyman "Cannonball" Titcomb's finest season. Titcomb was 14–8—nearly half his career 30 victories—with a 2.24 ERA.

Cy Seymour won 61 games in his first five years with the Giants, including a 25–19 season in 1898. That year he began to see more time in the outfield, however, and by 1900 he was

an established .300 hitter and gave up pitching altogether. Ed Doheny threw more than 900 innings from 1895 to 1901 but had only a 37–69 record to show for it.

George "Hooks" Wiltse won his first 12 decisions in 1904, which still stands as a record, equaled only once since. Known as Hooks for his fielding—not his nose or his curveball, as popular theories have it—Wiltse threw one of only five 10-inning no-hitters in major league history, blanking the Phillies at the Polo Grounds on July 4, 1908. He would have had a perfect game, except for grazing the opposing pitcher with two outs in the ninth; the Giants scored in the tenth to win 1–0. In 11 seasons, Wiltse and Christy Mathewson formed one of the most successful lefty–righty tandems in history, combining for 433 wins, behind only Eddie Plank and Chief Bender of the Philadelphia Athletics.

Hooks Wiltse, 1912

Rube Marquard, 1912

John McGraw brought on another lefty in 1908, paying $11,000 to sign Rube Marquard. By 1911 he and Matty were an even more formidable combo. On the pennant winners of 1911–1913, Marquard was 24–7, 26–11, and 23–10. The total of 73–28 included a record-tying 19 straight wins to start the 1912 season, the highlight of a Hall of Fame career.

It's a good thing Wiltse and Marquard won so many games, because another lefty on those teams, Leon "Red" Ames, virtually defined hard luck in those years and came to be known as Ka-lamity. Ames was working on a no-hitter in his big league debut in 1905 when the game was called in the fifth inning because of darkness. He threw 9⅓ no-hit innings on opening day in 1909 and then gave up six hits to ultimately lose 3–0 in 13 innings. He pitched brilliantly in the next two openers—carrying no-hitters into the eighth and seventh innings—and lost both of those as well. "Mac," he told manager John McGraw, "if I was to wear a

uniform trimmed with four-leaf clovers and a horseshoe in my glove, I couldn't win an opening game." Ames was also noted for his wildness, setting the post-1900 record with 30 wild pitches in 1905.

Art Nehf led the pitching staff on some of McGraw's greatest teams, and he won the seventh game of the World Series two years in a row, in 1921 and 1922. He also beat Walter Johnson in an epic 12-inning duel in Game One of the 1924 series, but the Senators won in seven. Nehf was 107–60 in eight years with the Giants.

The greatest Giants lefty of all-time, Carl Hubbell, threw a screwball reminiscent of Mathewson's fadeaway, and he bedeviled National League hitters for 16 years. He won two MVP Awards, in 1933, when he was 23–12 with a 1.66 ERA, and in 1936, when he was 26–6 with a 2.31 ERA. He not only equaled the record for 19 straight wins (set by Giants Tim Keefe and Marquard), but he topped it over two seasons, winning 24 straight. He threw the last Giant no-hitter at the Polo Grounds in 1929 and hurled an 18-inning shutout in 1933. His lifetime record of 253–154 put him in the Hall of Fame in 1947.

Dave Koslo topped .500 in only 3 of his 10 Giant seasons, even going 10–14 in 1949, when he led the league with a 2.50 ERA. Johnny Antonelli, newly acquired from the Braves, led the league with a 2.30 ERA in 1954 while throwing six shutouts en route a 21–7 record that helped secure the pennant. Antonelli was 108–84 in seven years with the Giants.

Two lefties named Billy—Pierce and O'Dell—joined with Juan Marichal and Jack Sanford in a formidable rotation for the 1962 pennant winners. O'Dell was a career best 19–14 that year. Pierce, 35, was near the end of a storied all-star career with the Chicago White Sox when the Giants got him, but he proved a vital cog, finishing 16–6. He was undefeated at Candlestick Park, and in the three-game playoff with the Dodgers, he won Game One and saved Game Three. Pierce lost a nail-biter in Game Three of the World Series to the Yankees, 3–2, but he took the must-win Game Six, 5–2—his thirteenth win of the year at the 'Stick.

Carl Hubbell, 1930s

Johnny Antonelli, late 1950s

Mike McCormick had led the league with a 2.70 ERA in 1960, but the Giants traded him in 1962 after three mediocre seasons. They brought him back in 1967 as a long reliever, and another pitcher's injury led to a spot start. Success begat success, and McCormick reeled off eight straight wins on his way to a league-leading 22–10 record and the first Cy Young Award in Giants history.

Ron "Bear" Bryant—named more for his bulky build than for the famed Alabama football coach—wasn't much of a star on the 1971 division champs, but he came into his own the next two years, chalking up records of 14–7 and 24–12, which still stands as the most wins in a season for a San Francisco southpaw. Bryant was almost as well known for his giant stuffed bear, complete with a uniform. But when he slipped on a slide in a spring training swimming pool, he needed 30 stitches and was never the same pitcher.

The back of the uniform said "Vida," and everyone knew who he was. Vida Blue had starred across the bay for the Oakland A's dynasty of the early 1970s, but he still had some gas in the tank when the Giants got him in 1978 for seven players and cash. He went 18–10 that year with a 2.79 ERA and was named *The Sporting News* National League Pitcher of the Year.

Bob Knepper also turned in a fine year in 1978 (17–11, 2.63 ERA) but spent his best years with Houston. Atlee Hammaker was an all-star for the Giants in 1983, leading the league with a 2.25 ERA and a phenomenal ratio of 127 strikeouts to 32 walks.

The Giants had success in the late 1980s and 1993 but did not boast a dominant lefty until Shawn Estes' 1997 season, when he was 19–5 with a 3.18 ERA. His ERA never again fell below 4.00, and even though he was 15–6 in 2000, he struggled to regain his old form.

Fan favorite Kirk "Woody" Rueter won in double-digits seven straight years. He was 16–9 in 1998, and his 14–8 mark in 2002 made him a stalwart of that pennant-winning staff.

Noah Lowry electrified the Giants in his rookie year of 2004, when he won his first six decisions, and then won his first

Vida Blue, circa 1985

Atlee Hammaker, 1990

Kirk Rueter, 2004

Barry Zito, 2009

decision in 2005 to run his career start to 7–0. He struggled that year but turned it around with a 5–0 record in August. He was 14–8 in 2007 but missed 2008 and 2009 due to injuries, putting his career in jeopardy.

In 2007 former Cy Young Award winner Barry Zito jumped across the bay, leaving the A's and joining the Giants for a record-setting sum. But he hasn't been the same pitcher since. He lost his first six starts of 2008 and led the league in losses with 17. He struggled again in 2009, but he showed some of his old self in the second half of the season.

In 2009 the Giants brought in the biggest left-hander of all: 6-foot-10, 45-year-old Randy Johnson—"the Big Unit"—a Bay Area native and winner of five Cy Young Awards. Johnson thrilled Giants fans when he won his 300th career game on June 4 over the Washington Nationals, only the sixth lefty in history to reach that milestone.

Jonathan Sanchez was a promising lefty who struggled so badly in 2009 that he was sent to the bullpen in June. But on July 10, Bruce Bochy needed a starter against the Padres at AT&T Park, and Sanchez stepped in and became the first Giants pitcher in more than 30 years to throw a no-hitter. In 2010, he went 13–9 with a 3.07 ERA and 205 strikeouts, and his win over the Padres on the final day of the season clinched the NL West title.

Madison Bumgarner came up from Fresno in 2010 as the Giants' fifth starter, and the 6-foot-5 farmboy never looked back. He was 7–6 with an ERA of 3.00 in the regular season, but it was the postseason where the rookie shined. He won the clinching Game Four against the Braves, turned in two clutch outings against the Phillies, and then won Game Four of the World Series with eight shutout innings. "I can't say enough about what he did tonight," manager Bruce Bochy said after the game. "I mean, a 21-year-old kid on that stage, pitching like that. He had it all working."

Doc Crandall, 1912

Jumbo Brown, with Dick Bartell, 1938

RELIEVERS

I n the nineteenth century, pitchers finished what they started. If they couldn't, sometimes a position player would. Giants outfielder Mike Tiernan tied for the league lead in saves in 1887—with one.

Then along came John McGraw, master tactician and baseball innovator. The custom at the time was to use a starting pitcher, often the ace, to finish up close games, and the Giants manager certainly did that. Witness Christy Mathewson's 29 career saves, or Joe McGinnity's 21. In 1904 and 1905, the Giants led the NL in saves, with 15 each year, while the next closest team recorded only 6.

McGraw's relievers were not just sore-arm starters, as with so many other managers. He'd use a different closer each year, such as Roscoe "Rubberlegs" Miller, Claude Elliott, or George

Malarkey. In 1909 he established the first pure reliever, Doc Crandall, who led the league in games finished with more than 20 in each of the next six seasons. Crandall recorded 24 saves in that period.

The save leaders remained ace starters for many years—Carl Hubbell led the league with eight saves in 1934—but relief specialists began to pop up here and there in the 1930s and 1940s. At 6-foot-4 and 295 pounds, the Giants' "Jumbo" Brown—some nicknames need no explanation—appeared in 146 games from 1938 to 1941, starting none, finishing 100, and saving 27.

In Ace Adams' six years with the Giants, all but 7 of his 302 appearances were in relief, and he registered 49 career saves, leading the league in 1944 and 1945. By 1950, when the Phillies' full-time reliever Jim Konstanty won the MVP Award, the relief pitchers' role was established.

World War II veteran Hoyt Wilhelm became the first Hall of Fame reliever. The knuckleball specialist started his career with the Giants in 1952 with a stunning 15–3 record, all in relief. He saved 41 games over five years for the Giants before going on to a 21-season, 227-save career. "He threw more strikes with that knuckleball than anybody I've ever seen," said Bobby Thomson.

Wilhelm was often paired in the bullpen with Marv Grissom, who from 1954 to 1958 won 27 games and saved 58. Grissom threw 2⅔ scoreless innings to get the win in Game One of the 1954 World Series.

It doesn't show up in the stats, but the 1954 series may have produced the best line any reliever ever uttered, if the story can be believed. In that first game at the Polo Grounds, with the score tied 2–2 in the eighth inning, the Indians had two men on and nobody out. A lefty, Don Liddle, was brought in to retire left-handed hitter Vic Wertz, who was already 3 for 3 with a triple. Wertz drove Liddle's first pitch 462 feet to the deepest part of the Polo Grounds, and center fielder Willie Mays, with his back to the plate, made perhaps the greatest catch in World Series history. Grissom came in to relieve Liddle, and Liddle told him, "Well, I got my man."

Wispy Stu Miller is best remembered for the wind blowing him into a balk in the 1961 All-Star Game at Candlestick Park, but he was a solid relief specialist in five seasons with the Giants. The junk-baller with bafflingly slow stuff led the league with a 2.47 ERA in 1958 and was 14–5 with a league-leading 17 saves in 1961. He saved 19 games on the 1962 NL champs.

Frank Linzy registered 21 saves in his rookie year of 1965 and was a steady pitcher until he was traded in 1970. Middle relievers were coming into vogue, and save leaders were starting to get into the 30s.

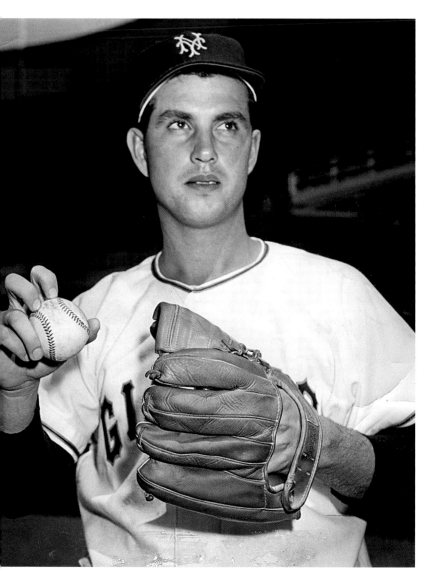

Hoyt Wilhelm, circa 1962

Stu Miller, 1961

Rod Beck, 1993 All-Star Game

The Giants boasted some impressive bullpens in the 1970s and 1980s. Randy Moffitt—perhaps best known as tennis star Billie Jean King's brother—teamed first with Elias Sosa and then with Gary Lavelle as potent relief combos. In 10 years with the team, Moffitt saved 83 games. Lavelle holds the team record for games by a pitcher, with 647, while Moffitt is fifth on that list with 459.

In his Giants career, Lavelle saved 127 games and recorded a 2.82 ERA. He also led a clubhouse Christian group in the 1980s that wasn't always popular but included players such as Jack Clark, Bob Knepper, and Rob Andrews.

With a stunning sinkerball, Greg Minton pitched in 552 games and saved 125 of them. Nicknamed Moon Man, Minton was the team flake. Minton and Lavelle used to keep warm on cold Candlestick nights by sitting in the sauna during games, coming out sweaty but ready to pitch.

The Giants had capable relievers in the 1980s, including Scott Garrelts, Mike LaCoss, Craig Lefferts, and Jeff Brantley. But it wasn't until Rod Beck's arrival that they had a bona fide shut-'em-down closer. The burly Beck saved 17 games in 1992 and then hit stardom in 1993 with a team-record-shattering 48 saves in 52 chances. He also notched 86 strikeouts in 78 innings with a 2.16 ERA. In seven years with the Giants, Beck saved 199 games. "Shooter" affected the look of an Old West gunslinger with his Fu Manchu mustache, and he threw a devastating split-fingered fastball.

The Giants brought in Robb Nen in 1998 and let Beck go. While Beck went on to save 51 games for the Cubs that year, Nen became the Giants' career saves leader, saving 206 games over five years. Another intimidator, Nen would enter during the "Nenth inning" to the tune of "Smoke on the Water" and routinely throw fastballs in the high 90-mph range. In 2000 he gave up only 11 earned runs in 66 innings, a 1.50 ERA, and in 2001 he led the league with 45 saves. He struck out 473 in 378.1 innings, but injuries prematurely ended his career.

In the Dusty Baker era, Giant fans loved to ride the manager for overusing his bullpen. The criticism reached its apotheosis in the 2002 World Series, when Baker removed Russ Ortiz with a 5–0 lead after a couple of hard hits in the seventh inning of Game Six, and the exhausted pen blew the game. First Felix Rodriguez, who had appeared in 71 games that year, surrendered a three-run home run to Scott Spiezio. Then Tim Worrell (80 games) got out of the inning but yielded a home run and two singles in the eighth. Finally Nen, who had pitched in 68 games and had a sore arm that would prevent him from ever pitching again after the series, gave up a game-winning double to Troy Glaus.

Brian Wilson took over the closer's job in 2008 and brought some serious heat. Sporting a jet-black beard, the colorful Wilson led the league with 48 saves in 2010, and fans quickly began pinning on their own facial hair and "Fear the Beard" T-shirts. The well-stocked bullpen was a key to the Giants' success, with Jeremy Affeldt, Sergio Romo, Ramon Ramirez, Javier Lopez, Santiago Casilla, and others playing key roles.

Robb Nen, 2002

Brian Wilson, 2010 World Series

UNIFORMS

John Montgomery "Monte" Ward's waxed mustache is not the only thing that tells you he lived in the nineteenth century: his baseball uniform looks nothing like those worn today. His cap is flat topped, with stripes circling it and a small bill. His short sleeved shirt has wide stripes, like a referee's, and is buttoned up to his neck. The pants go below the knees, and his belt appears heavy and wide. No name or number appears on the jersey.

Uniforms in the game's early decades went through many variations and styles, including ties, laces, or collars at the neck line, sleeves both long and short, socks of changing color and patterns, a multitude of caps—and on the players themselves, plenty of creative facial hair, from thin handlebar mustaches to thick muttonchops. By the turn of the century, teams adopted different uniforms for home and away. They typically wore wool and cotton flannel, which must have been horribly hot in the summer.

John McGraw took over as manager in 1902, and he appreciated dressing in style, but he was always uniformed like his players, a departure from the suit and top hat look of earlier manager Jim Mutrie.

The World Series was also something special for McGraw, and he had the Giants wearing black broadcloth uniforms in the 1905 World Series, when the team roared to victory. The next season he had "World Champions" emblazoned on the players' jerseys. Baseball being the most superstitious of sports, the Giants donned black again when they returned to the Fall Classic in 1911, though with less success.

The full city name ran across the chest in most years in the early 1900s, but by 1904 the home city's initials became the identifying mark, with an enormous N on the right breast and an equally bold Y on the left. Around 1908 the Giants adopted the familiar Old

John Montgomery Ward, 1880s

Mike Donlin, 1906

Art Fletcher, 1911 World Series

English "NY" logo. The logo initially was placed on the sleeve, with no lettering on the jersey front.

That logo changed only subtly over the years. From 1908 to 1916, and again from 1919 to 1922 and for the 1928 and 1929 seasons, the team used a black logo, with the serifs on three points of the *N* almost in a teardrop shape. In three other years in the 1920s and in 1930–1931, the same logo was used, only in orange. In 1948 the team adopted a narrower, more symmetrical logo.

Through about 1930, the NY logo appeared on home uniforms while the word *Giants* identified the team on the road. Eventually, the team nickname became standard at home while the city name, spelled out, ran across the chest of road uniforms.

Standard black pinstripes first appeared on Giants uniforms in 1911, but in the words of Baseball Almanac, "McGraw was quite unpredictable and often innovative in dictating the color schemes of his Giants." He introduced violet as a trim color in 1913 and candy-cane-striped socks in the 1920s. At one point the uniform had a fine cross-hatching, and in 1916 "bands of five thin purple stripes were perpendicularly intersected to create a near 'plaid' effect," with an oversized violet "NY" logo and old-fashioned pillbox cap.

The pinstripes lasted through the 1920s before giving way to solid white and gray. Blue caps, socks, and lettering made an appearance in the 1930s and 1940s, but by mid-century, the team adopted the traditional button-down flannels with the now-familiar black-and-orange color scheme.

Frankie Frisch, 1921

Joe McGinnity, 1904

Mel Ott, circa 1933

Sometimes when teams move, they take on new nicknames for their new cities. Although there was a history of San Francisco Seals in the Pacific Coast League, the Giants kept their name when they left New York for California. Aside from replacing the "NY" logo with an "SF," not much else changed.

But without "New Yawk speak," headline writers stopped calling them "the Jints." In more recent years, in tribute to many of their players' Latin American roots, they've played at least a game a year wearing "Gigantes" uniforms.

Baseball began to adopt synthetic materials in the 1960s, increasing players' comfort. In the late 1970s and early 1980s, the Giants switched to orange-and-black double knits, occasionally donning all-black uniforms with the team name in an orange script. The black uniforms made a return on some Friday games in 2001; Barry Bonds was wearing one when he hit his seventy-first home run.

In the 1990s, the road uniform sported the interlocking "SF" over the heart. The home uniform said "Giants" in all capital letters, with the G and S larger than the rest.

The team ultimately returned to tradition, with a cream-colored home uniform with "Giants" across the chest in orange and black, and gray road uniforms with "San Francisco" across

the chest. On the home jerseys, the typeface is more Victorian, while the road jerseys are a blocky sans serif style.

While baseball offers some flexibility, the Giants use fewer uniform variations than other teams. Most Giants wear their pants down to their cleats, but several, including Matt Cain, Barry Zito, and Nate Schierholtz, sport black socks over their calves.

In 2010, the Giants inaugurated "Orange Fridays," in which the team wore orange uniforms for Friday night home games.

The Giants have retired nine uniform numbers, in addition to Jackie Robinson's 42. The number 24 of Willie Mays is the only one honoring a player from both the New York and San Francisco Giants. From New York, Bill Terry (3), Mel Ott (4), Carl Hubbell (11), and Monte Irvin (20) are so honored. From San Francisco, no Giant will ever wear Juan Marichal's 27, Orlando Cepeda's 30, Gaylord Perry's 36, or Willie McCovey's 44. The wall honoring those legends also pays tribute to McGraw and Mathewson, from an era before uniforms bore numbers or names.

"You want to play for a team with a lot of tradition, and the Giants have one of the best traditions in baseball," shortstop Omar Vizquel said. "Just to wear that name, Giants, on your chest makes you feel like a Giant, even when you're only 5-foot-9."

Hoyt Wilhelm, circa 1954

Barry Zito, 2007

Willie McCovey, 1977

Will Clark, 1990

Interior view of the Polo Grounds, October 1910

THE BALLPARKS

Wealthy gentlemen in old New York once mounted ponies and played polo on a field at 110th Street and Sixth Avenue at the northern edge of Central Park. But when John B. Day, a Manhattan tobacco merchant, organized a baseball team and learned about the green from a shoeshine boy, the name Polo Grounds became forever associated with baseball.

Day's original team, the New York Metropolitans, used the field in 1880, helping prove that people would pay to watch the ball games. When the New York Gothams made their National League debut at the Polo Grounds in 1883, former president Ulysses S. Grant joined 15,000 others in watching them beat Philadelphia, 7–5, behind Hall of Fame right-hander Mickey Welch.

After the Giants won a championship in 1888, New York City confiscated the ball grounds site for redevelopment. In 1889 the team played a few games in Jersey City and Staten Island while waiting for completion of its new home, the second Polo Grounds. The field was in Harlem, at 155th Street and Eighth Avenue, on the southern half of what was known as Coogan's Hollow—the land at the base of a hillside known as Coogan's Bluff.

The Giants played only two seasons on that field. When the old Players League folded, the Giants bought the larger Brotherhood Park next door to the north, renamed it the Polo Grounds, and moved in for 1891. And there the team played for the next 67 years.

Actually, two ballparks stood on that site over the years: the original wooden stadium that the Giants moved into, which burned in a spectacular midnight fire in 1911, and the

rebuilt concrete-and-steel structure. The fire, most likely started when a discarded cigar smoldered among discarded papers and peanut shells, transfixed a throng of 10,000 fans and players. Damon Runyon mourned the loss of this "home of excitement; of some romance, and much baseball glory and achievement."

Construction started on the new park almost immediately, and the Giants went on two extended road trips and played some home games at Hilltop Park at 168th Street and Broadway, home of the American League's New York Highlanders, the team that would soon be renamed the Yankees. The Giants moved back into the Polo Grounds on June 28, before construction was fully complete. The park was dedicated on April 19, 1912.

Although the new park was ostensibly named for team owner John T. Brush, even at this early date the name Polo Grounds was seared onto New Yorkers' lips, and it was the Polo Grounds forever. While other fields of the era, such as Fenway Park in Boston, Wrigley Field in Chicago, and Ebbets Field in Brooklyn, were small and intimate, the Polo Grounds stood large and cavernous, shaped like a bathtub big enough to hold a battleship. Seating capacity had nearly doubled, from 17,300 to 34,000. Yet fans still loved its old-time charm and baseball atmosphere.

The Yankees played at the Polo Grounds from 1913 to 1922, ultimately moving after getting their eviction notice, when Babe Ruth arrived on the scene and turned the Yanks into winners and a big drawing card.

In 1923 a double-decked covered grandstand was added to the Polo Grounds, bringing capacity to 56,000. By the 1950s, however, the park showed its age. "The park was falling apart,"

Aerial view of the Polo Grounds

said fan Bob Leinweaver, who went to his first game at the Polo Grounds at age 11 in 1953. "The paint was peeling. And the paint was probably what was holding it up."

In 1957 owner Horace Stoneham grew frustrated with the sparse attendance and announced he was moving the team to San Francisco.

During the first few years on the West Coast, the Giants played in old Seals Stadium, a minor league park that previously housed the Pacific Coast League's legendary San Francisco Seals. Tucked into the Potrero Hill neighborhood at 16th and Bryant streets, Seals Stadium proved a much cozier home than the cavernous Polo Grounds. Even with a capacity of just 22,900, Seals Stadium managed to provide two of the Giants' best years in attendance to that point, topping one million both times.

Aerial view of Seals Stadium, April 1958

Aerial view of Candlestick Park, 1960

Two years was all the Giants had in Seals Stadium. By then, their new ballpark at Candlestick Point was built and ready for occupancy. But excitement for the new park never materialized into love for what quickly became a travesty. Even before the park was built, it appeared doomed. First came construction controversies involving contractor Charley Harney, who was sore that the park, located on his land, would not be named for him. He left things unfinished, including the heating system.

Chub Feeney, then vice president of the Giants, visited the construction site one afternoon. As Feeney recalled to writer Roger Angell, "he was almost blown out of the car, almost onto his back. He asked the foreman, 'Is it always this windy here?' And the foreman told him, 'Oh no, only between May and September, and only between 1 and 5 in the afternoon.'" Which happened to be the time of most baseball games.

Richard Nixon, then U.S. vice president, threw out the first pitch in 1960, declaring the park a gem. The story goes that the

Aerial view of AT&T Park, 2006

Candlestick wind blew Giants reliever Stu Miller off the mound in a 1961 All-Star Game; Miller says it just gave him a little sway, although enough that the umpire called a balk. Director of stadium operations Don Foreman called the wind the Hawk. San Francisco's freezing fog was a factor as well. Willie McCovey tells of hitting a routine fly ball that Duke Snider lost in the fog. By the time the ball landed and Snider found it, McCovey was on third with a triple. "That's the closest I ever came to hitting an inside-the-park home run," he said.

"They said it should be an advantage to us, that the other team was not used to it," said longtime second baseman Tito Fuentes. "That's what they said. But the other team came for three days and then got to leave. We had to be there for 81 days."

Owner Bob Lurie tried repeatedly to get a new home for the Giants. "We lost four elections, two in San Francisco and two down on the Peninsula, in San Jose and Santa Clara," Lurie said. "I got to the point where I wasn't going to stay at the 'Stick. It was a financial disaster. We did surveys to see why people weren't coming. Even on a beautiful, bright, sunny day in San Francisco, the 'Stick was foggy and cold. It was a tough sell."

Finally, new Giants ownership put together a privately financed deal to build a stadium closer to downtown, in San Francisco's China Basin. Pacific Bell Park opened to rave reviews in April 2000, not only because it was oriented away from the wind but also for its views of San Francisco Bay and downtown.

That park has had three names in its short life, owing to the fury of corporate mergers and acquisitions. It started as Pac Bell Park, named for the longtime northern California phone company. The name became SBC Park in 2004, when the former Southwestern Bell Company acquired Pacific Bell. That name morphed into AT&T Park in 2006, when that company merged with SBC. (Candlestick itself had become part of the corporate naming frenzy, going by 3Com Park in the Giants' final years and now by Monster Park, where the 49ers football team plays.)

If Yankee Stadium was the House That Ruth Built, then AT&T really ought to be named for Barry Bonds. The water alongside is named McCovey Cove, and Bonds put more home runs there than anyone. Plaques on the walkway along the cove commemorate Bonds' milestone home runs. A less controversial suggestion is offered by a popular San Francisco bumper sticker: "Say Mays Field."

Polo Grounds playing field, 1905

THE PLAYING FIELDS

The Giants have played on some of the most unusual fields in baseball.

When baseball first nosed out polo on the original Polo Grounds in 1883, the Gothams occupied the southeast corner and the Metropolitans played on the southwest corner.

In an 1886 double-header, word got out about the Giants' exciting 6–5 win in 10 innings in the opener, and 20,000 fans jammed the park for the nightcap. So many people stood on the outfield that the teams agreed that any ball into the crowd was a ground-rule single. The Giants lost 4–1.

In 1889 the Giants moved to a new field, also called the Polo Grounds. Most of their stars had joined a new Giants team in the upstart Players League and played in a stadium, Brotherhood Park, adjacent to the Polo Grounds. In an 1890 game called at the time the greatest ever played, 19-year-old Giants pitcher Amos Rusie dueled 20-year-old Boston Beaneater Kid Nichols in a scoreless tie into the thirteenth inning. When Mike Tiernan of the Giants hit a home run to win it, the crowds in both ballparks cheered loudly.

The next year the Giants moved to what would be their long-term home. At once both cozy and cavernous, the Polo Grounds featured short porches in right and left field extending out to what was, by modern standards, a preposterously deep center field. They moved in and out over the years, but the left field foul pole ranged only from 277 feet from home plate to 287 feet; right field's was 256 to 259. Center, which started at 433 feet out in 1911, was 505 feet away in the 1940s.

Polo Grounds playing field, 1954 World Series

Because of the unusual water tables beneath the playing field, the outfield sloped downward, until the ground was far deeper at the wall than it was in the infield. People in the dugout could see only the top half of the outfielders.

The short porch in left was where Bobby Thomson's home run landed. A few years later, minor leaguer Willie McCovey was shown the ballpark and told, "This is where you'll play for the rest of your life." According to writer Brian Murphy, McCovey said his eyes "lit up." But by the time McCovey hit the big leagues two years later, the Giants were in San Francisco.

At Seals Stadium, their first California home, the Giants had to adjust to more standard field dimensions. The foul poles were 90 feet farther away—361 feet in left, 350 feet in right—and center field was a more manageable 400 feet from home plate.

Candlestick Park opened with foul poles 330 feet away and a 420-foot center field. The power alleys of left- and right-center were 397 feet away. By the time the Giants left the park in 1999, center was 20 feet closer, and the alleys had moved in to 365 feet away while the foul poles shifted only slightly. A more distinguishing feature of the stadium was the large foul territory, which made it quite a pitchers' ballpark.

Candlestick had natural grass when it opened but switched to artificial turf in 1972 for football's 49ers. The Giants ripped it out and replaced it with grass before the 1979 season.

When the Giants opened their new ballpark at China Basin—then called Pac Bell Park, now AT&T Park—it had a smaller foul territory and a much more intimate feel. The backstop, 73 feet back at Candlestick originally (moved to 66 feet by 1999) is only 48 feet at AT&T.

While the right field foul pole at AT&T is an enticing 307 feet away, center field extends to 421 feet in what's become known as Triples Alley. The left field pole is 335 feet out.

AT&T also has asymmetrical dimensions and a brick wall and archways in right field, giving it a throwback look but making it one of the most difficult places to field in the major leagues. "The wall has so many different textures, surfaces, crevices, and corners that the ball just doesn't do the same thing every time," said former Giants outfielder Randy Winn, who knew the "Great Wall of China Basin" intimately.

Candlestick Park playing field, 1989

AT&T Park playing field, 2006

BILLBOARDS AND SCOREBOARDS

Advertising in the outfield is a long-standing baseball tradition. While people worry today about ballplayers as role models and their influence on children, baseball billboards have often promoted alcohol and tobacco. The Giants' outfield advertising has been no exception. The center field scoreboard at the Polo Grounds featured an enormous three-dimensional cigarette, the smoke billowing into the words "A hit!" and capital letters urging fans to "Always Buy Chesterfield." The *H* or *E* in the brand name would light up to indicate a hit or error. (When the Mets played at the Polo Grounds in 1962 and 1963, the sign advertised Rheingold beer.)

The most prominent promotion in the Polo Grounds was the Longines clock atop the center field scoreboard, 80 feet high at its peak. Longines watches were advertised on many such clocks in old ballparks, before digital clocks came into vogue.

Billboards once were plastered on the ballpark's outfield walls, but they were removed from the Polo Grounds in the 1940s, which also had the effect of evening out the left-center field wall. The wall had been 12 feet tall in some parts and 14, 16, and even 18 feet in others, depending on the size of the particular advertisements.

When the Giants arrived at Seals Stadium, a Longines clock adorned a light tower in left-center field, and a beef billboard topped the hand-operated scoreboard in center.

When Candlestick Park opened in 1960, it was the first ballpark with a modern scoreboard, then the biggest in baseball—94 feet high, 164 feet wide. The scoreboard had its own Longines clock and ads claiming, "Cars love Shell!" and, for Coca-Cola, "Be really refreshed!" The park was updated in 1972, and while efforts to tamp down the wind proved ineffective, bright new billboards were prevalent.

Pac Bell Park opened at the height of the dot-com era in 2000, right in the heart of San Francisco's South of Market neighborhood. Internet companies were spending money freely, and the ballpark benefited, until the dot-coms crashed.

Every cup holder at every seat bore a Webvan logo, but the company went bankrupt in 2001 and its decals were eventually removed or covered over.

Fortunately, other advertisers are more durable. Fans decried the commercialism of letting Coca-Cola erect an enormous bottle in left field, but slides in the Coke bottle have proven a major attraction in the park's Fan Lot, where young children while away the game.

The Chevron billboards along the left field wall often provide a landmark for announcers, and Levi's Landing in right field pays tribute to a San Francisco icon.

Tobacco ads no longer have a place in the ballpark, and some of the signs reflect healthier times, particularly billboards for Catholic Healthcare West (CHW).

Billboards and scoreboard, Polo Grounds, 1911

Chesterfield cigarettes billboard, Polo Grounds, 1950

Before the 2007 season, AT&T Park installed a $3 million high-definition scoreboard, one of the first three in a U.S. sports stadium. It offers not only beautiful video and replays but also terrific updates on the action. The Mitsubishi Electric Diamond Vision scoreboard is 31½ feet high by 103 feet wide, lit up by 3 million LEDs. It replaced an old Panasonic Astrovision screen.

The new scoreboard fits with the high-tech nature of AT&T Park, which has offered free Wi-Fi since 2004, mounted 225 flat-screen high-definition televisions throughout the ballpark in 2006, and installed hundreds of solar panels to provide energy in 2007. In addition, it's a perfect complement to the retro hand-operated scoreboard in right-center field that updates major league action.

Scoreboard, Candlestick Park, 1960

Scoreboard and billboards, AT&T Park, 2010

BULLPENS, DUGOUTS, AND CLUBHOUSES

Polo Grounds dugout, 1954

I n modern times, baseball teams' clubhouses are connected to the dugouts, affording players an easy exit or even escape during a game. But in the Polo Grounds, the clubhouse was in center field, more than a football field away from the dugout.

The Polo Grounds' clubhouse was built in 1923, rising three stories. Joshua Prager offered a vivid description in *The Echoing Green*, his book about Bobby Thomson's home run: In the locker room, each player had a rectangular wooden cubby, separated by wire mesh and open-faced, with his name written on a strip of adhesive tape. Adjacent to that was the trainer's room, with its whirlpools and massage tables.

Bathrooms and showers were upstairs, along with clubhouse man Eddie Logan's vast supply of hair cream, aftershave, and other toiletries. Up another shorter set of stairs was a players' lounge, with card tables, two sand-filled stone tubs where players snuffed their cigarettes, and coolers full of soda, beer, and juice, and ice with an ice pick. On the wall, Logan kept

Candlestick Park clubhouse, 1960

AT&T Park dugout, 2007

the "gyp sheet": a roster where he kept track of who owed how much for the drinks.

Logan also kept other supplies there, from balls and gloves to chewing tobacco. Off this lounge was the manager's office, where Leo Durocher had a glass-topped mahogany desk and a bar stocked for reporters. The visiting clubhouse, merely a locker room and lounge, stood behind Durocher's office, accessible by stairs from center field.

Up yet one more flight of stairs were the executive offices of Giant owner Horace Stoneham and other team officials, and a press lounge. At the base of the clubhouse was a row of windows that were technically in play, although no batted ball ever reached that far in nearly 50 years.

The Polo Grounds featured bullpens in fair territory—the only ones in play in the major leagues, albeit 450 feet from home plate. Prager went into immaculate detail in his book to describe the Giants' ambitious scheme in 1951: to plant a spy in the center field clubhouse with a telescope to steal opponents' signs and to relay those signs via a buzzer to the bullpen. There, a backup catcher could relay the signs to the batter or to the dugout, where someone close to the batter could send the signal.

Many players froze in the dugouts over the years at Candlestick Park, but at least the bullpens were now in foul territory.

AT&T Park clubhouse, 2004

At AT&T Park, everything is built for comfort. The players have a spacious clubhouse—best known as the spot where Barry Bonds maintained his own empire, with a lounge chair, television, and extra lockers. A short corridor leads directly to an underground batting cage, and it's up a few steps and you're in a roomy dugout. The bullpens remain close to the field in foul territory, where fans can get a good glimpse as pitchers get warmed up.

Giants Fans and Knothole Gangs

I n the team's earliest incarnation, the Gothams drew a high-
class crowd. Former president Ulysses S. Grant attended
their first game in 1883.

    With owner John B. Day a successful businessman,
the Giants could count on a Wall Street fan base. Their first hero
was slugger Roger Connor, whom they called Dear Old Roger.
In a game in 1888, Connor launched a blast that sailed out of the
Polo Grounds and onto 112th Street beyond right field. To show
their appreciation, stockbrokers at the game passed a top hat
around and collected enough to buy Connor a $500 gold watch
at Tiffany's.

    Manager Jim Mutrie often sat in the stands in his black top
hat, formal black coat and cravat, and waxed mustache, hustling
up and down the aisles yelling, "Who are the people?" The fans

Fans at the Polo Grounds, October 8, 1908

Fans lining up for World Series tickets at the Polo Grounds, October 1911

Fans at AT&T Park, August 2009

would shout back, "We are the people!" And everyone would sing the Giants' battle anthem.

After moving several times in their first 28 seasons, the Giants settled into the Polo Grounds at 155th Street, a part of Harlem known as Coogan's Hollow. And while the hollow helped give the ballpark its unusual oval shape, Coogan's Bluff just beyond left field helped define its location for nearly half a century—and gave fans a place to sneak a free peak into the ballpark.

When the Giants and Cubs had to replay the infamous "Merkle's Boner" game of 1908, an estimated 250,000 people showed up. The park itself couldn't even hold 50,000, and the masses trying to storm the gates were scattered. About 40,000 remained, however, to watch the game from Coogan's Bluff and from the tops of telephone poles, trees, and subway platforms. One man, firefighter Henry T. McBride, fell from a pillar on the elevated train platform and was killed. The Giants lost the game.

That was in the old, wooden Polo Grounds, before the grandstand obstructed many of the views. Renovations in 1911 and 1923 took away most of the sight lines but still left enough for some fans. Often a portable radio helped complete the picture.

One feature of the Polo Grounds, and many other old ballparks, that seems odd in today's security-conscious environment, was that fans could walk across the field after the game on their way out. Everyone usually behaved well, but after the final game in New York in 1957, the players knew the crowd—albeit fewer than 11,000—was angry and looking for souvenirs. The players sprinted for the clubhouse, and the fans staged a near-riot, tearing up the turf, ripping apart anything they could get their hands on, and calling for the head of owner Horace Stoneham, the man behind the decision to move the team.

To this day, some diehard fans back in New York still follow the team and maintain a New York Baseball Giants Nostalgia Society.

Fans welcomed the Giants to San Francisco with a parade, but they had an uneasy relationship with the team in those early years. It was as if San Franciscans were inheriting someone else's squad, and it took awhile to make it their own. "This is the damnedest town," wrote Frank Conniff while covering a visit to San Francisco by Soviet premier Nikita Khrushchev. "They cheer Khrushchev and boo Willie Mays."

Mays was New York's hero, and San Franciscans first adopted Orlando Cepeda and Willie McCovey as their icons. When the Giants won the pennant in Los Angeles in 1962, so many fans thronged the airport that McCovey and Cepeda had to hitchhike home. When they got to their shared apartment, the neighborhood was out in force, throwing them a party.

Fans lining up for World Series game, October 2002

The fans came around to love Mays as well, of course. And they froze along with the team through the indignities of Candlestick Park. "I really admire the fans," said Tito Fuentes. "They went there every day to suffer."

Well, some of them. Most stayed away in droves. In the lean years of losing teams, the Giants barely drew any crowds. In 1974 attendance hit an all-time low of 519,991—an average of 7,027 per game. The team, frustrated with the park, nearly moved to Toronto in 1976 and then—four failed ballot measures later—nearly moved to Florida in 1992.

"You have to feel for people who are Giants fans," said team executive Pat Gallagher. "They had to put up with Candlestick. And then they had to put up with the fear of the team leaving a couple of times." (Corny joke of the era: Why was Candlestick Park so windy? All those Giant fans.)

Gallagher said that the team faced a conundrum. On the one hand, it had to tell people how terrible the ballpark was, in hopes that they would help build a new one. On the other hand, it had to persuade people to attend games at that terrible ballpark. Gallagher helped walk that line by coming up with some innovative promotions, from the Croix de Candlestick awarded to every fan who sat through an extra-inning night game, to television

Fans keeping warm, Seals Stadium, April 1958

Fans viewing World Series game from Coogan's Bluff, Polo Grounds, October 1905

ads that mocked the park's reputation by showing fans trudging through the snow as if Candlestick were set in Valley Forge.

Gallagher's message: "It took guts to be a Giants fan. You couldn't buy it. You had to earn it."

Only three times did the Giants ever top 2 million fans at Candlestick: the pennant-winning year of 1989, the 103-win season of 1993, and the final year, 1999, when the Giants told fans to "tell it goodbye."

Starting in 2000, the Giants routinely drew more than 3 million fans a year to Pacific Bell/SBC/AT&T Park, even though the new park's capacity of 41,915 was dwarfed by Candlestick's 63,000.

Gallagher figures the lovely new ballpark is the karmic reward for fans who served time at the 'Stick.

The Giants also revived the old tradition inspired by Coogan's Bluff by creating spots from which fans can get a peek at the action inside the ballpark. Archways in the right-field wall afford free views under the stands from the walkway along McCovey Cove. Fans are asked to move along if it's crowded, but the "knot-hole" views have even been open during the World Series and All Star Game. The area is shaded and offers a player's-eye view of the action.

The Giants call the area's denizens the Knothole Gang and say the perk is unique in the major leagues, a throwback to Norman Rockwell paintings of kids peering at the action through holes in a fence. And when the Dodgers come to town, the gang can razz the opponent even more effectively than paying fans.

"We love to heckle the right fielder," fan John McKenney told the *Los Angeles Times*. "He may act like he can't hear us, but he hears us, all right. We give him tips on how to improve his game. And his hygiene."

The Giants' most devoted fan had to be Marjorie Wallace, who often left for the ballpark nine hours early, taking three buses to get there from her subsidized apartment. "Ballpark Marge" latched onto the team from its arrival in 1958 until her death in 2003. A seat outside the clubhouse was reserved for the "number one fan," and she greeted all the players. "She represented what a true fan was," J. T. Snow said.

Although attendance lagged when the team stopped winning, fans turned out in droves for the pennant drive in 2010. Wearing panda hats, Brian Wilson beards, Tim Lincecum wigs, and every shade of orange, they sang old Journey songs until they were hoarse and willed the Giants to the long-overdue championship.

Fans viewing game through archways in right-field wall, AT&T Park, 2004

Food at the Ballpark

What is a ballpark experience without food? And what would food at the ballpark have been without the Giants?

The Polo Grounds, after all, was the first major league park where Cracker Jack was sold. And the snack is forever associated with baseball thanks to "Take Me Out to the Ball Game," a song that Jack Norwirth wrote on the subway riding past the Polo Grounds.

Of all things, it was a British immigrant who legend has it sold the first hot dogs at a baseball game, two things that go together like America and apple pie. Unfortunately, a great deal of research into the origins of the hot dog has poked a hole in the myth, but it's still worth noting for its ubiquity and for the irrefutable fact that the man behind it, Harry M. Stevens, went on to lasting fame as the country's foremost ballpark concessionaire.

After arriving in the United States, Stevens started selling ice cream and soda at ball games and even sold rosters to fans, touting them by saying, "You can't tell the players without a scorecard." Stevens also promoted a tale that on a cold day in April 1901, at a Giants game at the Polo Grounds, he couldn't sell any ice cream and ordered his staff to round up "dachshund sausages," stuff them into bread rolls, and hawk them by hollering, "Get your red hots!" In the story, a newspaper cartoonist who couldn't spell *dachshund* memorialized them as "hot dogs," and the rest is history.

The only problem is, scholars have found earlier references to the term *hot dog*, and it may even refer to a common belief that dog meat was included in some sausages.

In the modern era, hot dogs are still a favorite at the ballpark, but food has risen to new levels. The offerings at AT&T Park are vast, but the most popular can be summed up in two words:

Beer server, AT&T Park, 2006

Derby Grill concessions stand, AT&T Park, 2006

garlic fries. The concessions selling the sticky, stinky, tasty fries became so popular that the Giants added six more stands in 2005.

Orlando Cepeda sometimes works the grill at Orlando's Barbecue, where fans devour Caribbean fare such as Baby Bull tri-tip sandwiches and cha-cha bowls, which contain jerk chicken and black beans on rice with pineapple relish. Krispy Kreme doughnuts were a big hit in the park's first seasons but have since given way to stands selling Sheboygan bratwursts, Tres Agaves tacos, and McCovey's pulled pork sandwiches.

Fans enjoying hot dogs, AT&T Park, 2006

SPORTSWRITERS

Baseball needed promotion in its early days, and the burgeoning New York press corps needed entertainment to feed its readers. From such necessities are beautiful friendships formed.

The Giants of John McGraw were covered by a talented crew of writers, several of whom won the Hall of Fame's J. G. Taylor Spink Award "for meritorious contributions to baseball writing": Damon Runyon, Sid Mercer, Heywood Broun, and Frank Graham were among the boys in the press box in those days.

Runyon, who went on to chronicle the characters of New York's underground so effectively that they were immortalized in *Guys and Dolls*, broke in as a Giants beat writer in 1911. When the ballpark burned that year, Runyon memorialized it in the *New York American*: "It means the Big Town; it means the Big City club; it is all the lights of Broadway and the lure of Gotham summed up in two words. . . . It is a place of surpassing magnificence, sparkling beneath the silver sun like a great green jewel, and best of all, it is the abiding place of the Giants!"

Press row at the Polo Grounds, 1913 World Series

Press box at the Polo Grounds, 1956

Media swarms around Barry Bonds at AT&T Park, 2007

Graham's coverage stretched from McGraw to Leo Durocher; Graham is credited as the reporter who first published Durocher's "nice guys finish last" comment, made when the Lip was a Dodger manager deriding Mel Ott and the Giants.

Writer Franklin Adams won fame for his poem "Baseball's Sad Lexicon," which immortalized the way the Chicago Cubs' double-play combo of Joe Tinker to Johnny Evers to Frank Chance bedeviled the Giants in the early part of the century—"ruthlessly pricking our gonfalon bubble, turning each Giant hit into a double."

Over the years, other great New York writers chronicling the Giants' exploits included Grantland Rice, Red Smith, and Arthur Daley. Pounding on a press box typewriter for the *New York Herald Tribune* on October 3, 1951, having just witnessed Bobby Thomson's home run, Smith wrote: "Now it is done. Now the story ends. And there is no way to tell it. The art of fiction is dead.

Nick Peters receives J. G. Taylor Spink Award

Reality has strangled invention. Only the utterly impossible, the inexpressibly fantastic, can ever be plausible again."

Roger Angell, the dean of contemporary baseball writers with his elegant columns in *The New Yorker*, was a lifelong Giant fan. His essays on the team's departure from New York were both celebratory and poignant. In "Farewell, My Giants" in *Holiday* magazine, his eulogistic look at the team's triumphs and tragedies ended at the last game at the Polo Grounds. As he left with his young daughter, Angell wrote, "I didn't feel anything—nothing at all. I guess I just couldn't believe it. But it's true, all right. The flags are down, the lights in the temple are out, and the Harlem River flows lonely to the sea."

The crew was no less distinguished when the Giants moved west.

Charles Einstein covered the Giants in New York—he was in the press box for Bobby Thomson's home run and Willie Mays' rookie year—and moved to San Francisco for a job at the *Examiner* as the Giants beat writer. He went on to write two books with Mays, as well as a memoir, *Willie's Time*.

Bob Stevens of the *San Francisco Chronicle* is another Spink Award winner. Among his more memorable phrases, he described a Mays triple in the 1959 All-Star Game this way: "The only man who could have caught that ball, hit it."

Nick Peters has not missed a San Francisco Giants home opener since 1958, and he covered the team from 1961 until he retired in 2007. He has written or coauthored some of the most definitive books on the team.

While newspapers' difficulties have caused dwindling attendance in many press boxes, many fine beat writers still follow today's Giants. They include Henry Schulman and John Shea of the *San Francisco Chronicle* and Andrew Baggarly of the *San Jose Mercury News*.

VOICES OF THE GIANTS

Radio has such a vital impact on the way so many people experience baseball that it's hard to believe the sport's owners once tried to keep the broadcasts from happening. Through the 1930s, teams feared that putting games on the radio would have a deleterious effect on attendance.

But in 1939, Larry MacPhail—who had pioneered radio broadcasts in Cincinnati—brought Red Barber to Brooklyn, and all New York teams followed suit. Within 10 years, broadcasting had entered its golden age, and the Giants were right there, with Russ Hodges and Ernie Harwell calling Giant games. Harwell—who became a legend with the Detroit Tigers—called Bobby Thomson's home run for NBC television, but it's Hodges' call that lives on as probably the most memorable baseball moment broadcast on the radio: "There's a long drive . . . it's going to be . . . I believe . . . THE GIANTS WIN THE PENNANT! THE GIANTS WIN THE PENNANT! THE GIANTS WIN THE PENNANT!

THE GIANTS WIN THE PENNANT! Bobby Thomson hits into the lower deck of the left field stands and the Giants win the pennant! And they're going crazy! They're going crazy! Waaa-hooo!"

Hodges' score sheet from that game is on display at the Hall of Fame; it's probably no surprise that he never actually wrote in Thomson's home run.

Hodges moved west with the team and formed a tandem with Lon Simmons. Although he slipped and called Seals Stadium "the Polo Grounds" in his broadcast of the first game on the West Coast, and occasionally lapsed and said "New York Giants," he grew to be beloved in San Francisco for his exuberant home run calls of "It's bye-bye, baby." The phrase found its way into the Giants' theme song.

Simmons had his own home run call, "You can tell it good-bye," which the Giants later adopted as their fond farewell to Candlestick.

Russ Hodges, with Willie Mays, 1966

Lon Simmons, 2002

Hank Greenwald, 1996

Renel Brooks-Moon, 2002 World Series

When the Giants moved to California, Les Keiter kept the team alive for its New York fans with three years of broadcasts. He read telegraph reports and re-created the games, hitting a drumstick on a wooden block to simulate the sound of a bat striking a ball.

Giants broadcasts became fairly vital to San Francisco as well. Once, when legendary *San Francisco Chronicle* columnist Herb Caen drove into the city's Broadway tunnel, the Giants were leading 4–2. When he emerged on the other side, they had lost 6–4 and he had missed a game-winning grand slam. He lobbied for months and ultimately had a wire put inside the tunnel to keep the games on the car radio.

Broadcaster Hank Greenwald was a popular quipster in the 1980s and 1990s. Once, when Houston's Ken Caminiti had to leave the game with a stomach ache, Greenwald said, "It seems only right that the guy with all the hits and RBIs should also have the runs."

When a local syndicate formed to buy the Giants, KNBR radio signed on and remains a part owner of the team, as is television station KTVU.

Jon Miller grew up a Giants fan but became a premier broadcaster in Baltimore. In 1997 the Giants brought him home, cementing a first-rate crew that handles games on KNBR and Comcast SportsNet Bay Area/NBC. Miller's baritone and skills as a raconteur earned him the Ford C. Frick Award in 2010 and induction into the Hall of Fame.

Miller is complemented by Dave Flemming and two of the most knowledgeable former ballplayers in the booth, "Kruk and Kuip," former Giants Mike Krukow and Duane Kuiper, who were teammates in San Francisco in the early 1980s. Krukow in particular has captivated fans with his own peculiar brand of baseball speak, exemplified when he tells a player to sit down after a poor showing: "Grab some pine, meat." And Kuiper defined the Giants when he hung the "torture" tag on them in 2010.

Erwin Higueros and former Giant Tito Fuentes handle the Spanish broadcasts.

The real voice of the Giants, however, is Renel Brooks-Moon, a radio personality known widely by her first name who has served as the public address announcer ever since AT&T Park opened. The Giants had already made history by making Sherry Davis the first woman PA announcer at Candlestick in 1992, and Renel took over seven years later with her distinct enunciations. When you hear every syllable of "An-dres Tor-res," you know Renel is in the house.

SPRING TRAINING

Willie Mays stretching at spring training, Phoenix, March 1961

I n the early part of the century, the Giants moved their spring facilities every few years. They trained in New York from 1900 to 1903, then in Savannah, Georgia, until 1905, and then in Memphis and even Los Angeles the next two years. In each place, John McGraw was frustrated that he couldn't keep his players' attention focused on baseball and preparing for the battles of the upcoming season.

That is until he found the perfect spot: Marlin Springs, Texas, a town with no distractions whatsoever.

The Giants trained in Marlin Springs from 1908 to 1918. "They thought that in a little town like that, they could keep the fellows under control better," Fred Snodgrass told Lawrence Ritter in *The Glory of Their Times*. Twice a day, the players would walk two miles along railroad tracks from the hotel to the ballpark.

Snodgrass said that spring training "was simpler, and it was tougher" in those days, compared to modern spring training with trainers and calisthenics and sophisticated machinery. (And that book came out in 1966.) "We didn't have 10 coaches, each a professional teacher in some aspect of baseball," Snodgrass said. "We had one old-timer, Arlie Latham, who had been a first-rate ballplayer and who was a fine fellow, but who was probably the worst third base coach who ever lived."

McGraw drove the team through running, batting practice, and fielding practice. In 1911 he even brought his own umpire to Texas on the notion that the locals he had hired were too inept

to adequately prepare the team for the season. McGraw seemed to view the spring as a time to train his managerial invective, and after he vociferously argued a safe call at first base in an intrasquad game, the umpire quit and left town.

From 1918 to 1931, the Giants trained either in San Antonio, Sarasota, or Gainesville, Florida, with one season in Augusta, Georgia. They continued an itinerant schedule through the 1930s and 1940s in places from Los Angeles to Miami Beach, even spending spring in oddball cities such as Havana, Cuba; Baton Rouge, Louisiana; and Lakewood, New Jersey.

In 1947 they settled in Phoenix, where—except for one year, 1951 in St. Petersburg—they stayed until moving to neighboring Scottsdale in 1982. In the early 1960s, Horace Stoneham built a $2 million development, Casa Grande, where the Giants could live and train during the spring, although they still played most of their games in nearby Phoenix. He planned for the facility to serve as a year-round resort, with hotel and golf course, but the freeway he thought would run by it was routed farther to the east, and the development wound up adding to his financial woes.

In 1992 the Giants opened a beautiful new stadium in Scottsdale that holds 12,000 people.

Spring training is, as always, a place to get in shape—unless you were an otherworldly athlete like Willie Mays. "He didn't do anything during the offseason," said Willie McCovey. "I'd go to his house, and he'd be in the bedroom, watching TV, or he'd drag you to the pool hall. And then on the first day of spring training, he'd look like it was mid-season. I knew darn well he hadn't been working out. The rest of us are huffing and puffing, and he's running around. He just had something about him that the rest of us didn't have."

Giants pitchers warming up at spring training, Louisiana, March 1934

Manager John McGraw addresses his players during spring training, Marlin Springs, Texas, circa 1914

Manager Roger Craig addresses his players during spring training, Scottsdale, Arizona, February 1986

Giants–Dodgers spring training game, Scottsdale Stadium, February 2009

Willie Mays of the Minneapolis Millers, 1951

Baseball did not have a formal farm system until Branch Rickey established it with the Cardinals in the 1920s, but minor league baseball had been around much longer than that. The Giants did have some early relationships with minor league teams, working in 1932 with a class-A team in Bridgeport, Connecticut, and a pair of rookie or class-B teams in North Carolina, the Winston-Salem Twins and the High Point Pointers.

Once the Dodgers started using their minor league affiliates to develop and promote talent, the Giants quickly followed suit. The Giants maintained a AAA team, the Minneapolis Millers, from 1946 to 1957. As the Giants pondered leaving New York, owner Horace Stoneham originally had his sights set on Minneapolis, until Walter O'Malley convinced him to join the Dodgers in California and keep the rivalry alive. In 1957 the Giants gave Minneapolis to the Red Sox in exchange for the San Francisco Seals, enabling the Giants to move west.

The Giants of that era developed one of baseball's elite farm systems, bringing along players such as Willie McCovey, Orlando Cepeda, Felipe Alou, and Jim Davenport.

The Giants also had minor league squads in Jersey City, New Jersey, from 1937 to 1945, the last stop before New York for players such as Monte Irvin.

The Giants maintained a AAA team in Phoenix from 1966 to 1997, at which point they moved their affiliation to a team closer to home, the Fresno Grizzlies. With the Giants' renewed emphasis on homegrown talent in recent years, rather than the veteran help brought in during the Barry Bonds era, Fresno has exhibited many impressive young stars, including Tim Lincecum, Matt Cain, Buster Posey, and Madison Bumgarner. Fresno manager Steve Decker is a fixture in San Francisco newspapers, giving the rundown on the latest prospect to get promoted.

Posey, the team's top draft pick from 2008, tore up the Pacific Coast League in early 2010, batting .349 in 49 games for Fresno before getting the call to join the big league club. Brandon Belt, a first baseman from Texas, may be the next great thing to come out of the farm system after batting a combined .352 at A, AA, and AAA in 2010.

In addition to Fresno, the Giants' minor league teams include, in AA, the Richmond (Va.) Flying Squirrels; in class A, the San Jose Giants, the Augusta GreenJackets in Georgia and the Salem-Keizer Volcanoes in Oregon (managed since 2008 by former big league skipper Tom Trebelhorn); in rookie ball, the Arizona Giants and the Dominican Summer League Giants.

*San Jose Giants players sign
autographs for fans, 1988*

*Fresno Grizzlies second
baseman Ivan Ochoa turns
a double play during spring
training game, 2008*

BIBLIOGRAPHY AND RESOURCES

Books and Articles

Angell, Roger. "The Companions of the Game." Chap. 12 in *Five Seasons: A Baseball Companion*. New York: Simon and Schuster, 1977.

———. "Farewell, My Giants!" *Holiday*, May 1958.

Bitker, Steve. *The Original San Francisco Giants: The Giants of '58*. Champaign, IL: Sports Publishing, 1998.

Brody, Tom C. "A Miller-hiller-haller-holler-lujah Twist." *Sports Illustrated*, September 17, 1962.

Carminati, Mike. "Welcome to the Halls of Relief: An Historical Overview of Relief Pitching." *SABR 36*, June 29, 2006.

Cepeda, Orlando, with Herb Fagen. *Baby Bull: From Hardball to Hard Time and Back*. Dallas: Taylor Publishing Co., 1998.

Chadwick, Bruce, and David M. Spindel. *The Giants: Memories and Memorabilia from a Century of Baseball*. New York: Abbeville Press, 1993.

Conrad, Barnaby, ed. *The World of Herb Caen: San Francisco, 1938–1997*. San Francisco: Chronicle Books, 1997.

Deford, Frank. *The Old Ball Game: How John McGraw, Christy Mathewson and the New York Giants Created Modern Baseball*. New York: Grove Press, 2005.

Einstein, Charles. *Willie's Time: A Memoir*. New York: J. B. Lippincott Co., 1979.

Eskenazi, Gerald. *The Lip: A Biography of Leo Durocher*. New York: William Morrow and Co., 1993.

Fainaru-Wada, Mark, and Lance Williams. *Game of Shadows: Barry Bonds, BALCO, and the Steroids Scandal That Rocked Professional Sports*. New York: Gotham Books, 2006.

Fimrite, Ron. "Gone With the Wind? The Giants Want out of Blustery Candlestick Park, and One of These Days They Just Might Get Their Wish." *Sports Illustrated*, September 1, 1986.

Fost, Dan. "Lords of No Rings." *San Francisco Magazine*, April 2008.

Glionna, John M. "Throwback at the Ol' Ballpark." *Los Angeles Times*, June 10, 2001.

Goldstein, Richard. "Les Keiter, Announcer Who Recreated Giants Games, Dies at 89." *New York Times*, April 15, 2009.

———. "Ruben Gomez, 77, Former Giants Pitcher." *New York Times*, July 30, 2004, A16.

Gray, Sid. "The Giants of Yesterday Bid Polo Grounds Farewell." *New York Herald Tribune*, September 30, 1957.

Greenwald, Hank. *This Copyrighted Broadcast*. San Francisco: Woodford Press, 1999.

Haft, Chris. "Kent Has Permanent Place in SF History." MLB.com, January 22, 2009. http://mlb.mlb.com/news/article.jsp?ymd=20090122&content_id=3762828&vkey=news_mlb&fext=.jsp&c_id=mlb

Hano, Arnold. *A Day in the Bleachers*. Cambridge, MA: Da Capo Press, 1995.

Hynd, Noel. *The Giants of the Polo Grounds: The Glorious Times of Baseball's New York Giants*. New York: Doubleday, 1988.

Irvin, Monte, with James A. Riley. *Nice Guys Finish First*. New York: Carroll and Graf Publishers, 1996.

Jensen, Don. "John McGraw." *Baseball Biography Project*. http://bioproj.sabr.org/bioproj.cfm?a=v&v=l&pid=9279&bid=983

Johanson, Matt. *Game of My Life: Memorable Stories of Giants Baseball*. Champaign, IL: Sports Publishing, 2007.

Krentzman, Jackie. "The Brick Monster, AKA the Right Field Wall." *Giants Magazine*, April 2009.

Lee, Ellen. "Giants Score Big: Club to Unveil Huge Hi-Def Scoreboard." *San Francisco Chronicle*, March 26, 2007.

Mathewson, Christy. "Why We Lost Three Championships." *Everybody's Magazine*, October 1914.

Mays, Willie, as told to Charles Einstein. *Willie Mays: My Life In and Out of Baseball*. New York: E. P. Dutton & Co., 1966.

Mays, Willie, with Lou Sahadi. *Say Hey*. New York: Simon and Schuster, 1988.

Megdal, Howard. *The Baseball Talmud: The Definitive Position-by-Position Ranking of Baseball's Chosen Players*. New York: HarperCollins Publishers, 2009.

Murphy, Brian. *San Francisco Giants: 50 Years*. San Rafael, CA: Insight Editions, 2008.

Newhouse, Dave. "A Memorial to Giants' No. 1 Fan." *Oakland Tribune*, June 29, 2003.

Neyer, Rob. *Rob Neyer's Big Book of Baseball Lineups*. New York: Fireside Books, 2003.

Okrent, Daniel, and Harris Lewine, eds. *The Ultimate Baseball Book*. Boston: Houghton Mifflin Co., 1991.

Olbermann, Keith. "The Goof That Changed the Game." *Sports Illustrated*, September 23, 2008.

Ortiz, Jorge L. "Alou Offended by Radio Host." *San Francisco Chronicle*, August 6, 2005, D1.

Peters, Nick. *Tales from the Giants Dugout*. Champaign, IL: Sports Publishing, 2003.

Plaschke, Bill. "A Turn for the Worse—Ten Years Ago, Bonds Added Smirk and Spin to a Homer Against Dodgers, a Twist with Long-Reaching Effects." *Los Angeles Times*, July 31, 2007.

Prager, Joshua. *The Echoing Green: The Untold Story of Bobby Thomson, Ralph Branca and the Shot Heard Round the World*. New York: Pantheon Books, 2006.

Puff, Richard A. "Silent George Burns: A Star in the Sunfield." *SABR Research Journal Archive*. http://research.sabr.org/brj/index.php/silent-george-burns-a-star-in-the-sunfield

Purdy, Mark. "For Giants, Blame the Curse of Sal Maglie." *San Jose Mercury News*, October 4, 2001.

Ritter, Lawrence S. *The Glory of Their Times: The Story of the Early Days of Baseball Told by the Men Who Played It*. New York: Macmillan, 1966.

Sabino, David. "Alou You Need to Know." *Sports Illustrated*, June 9, 2003.

Schechter, Gabriel. *Victory Faust: The Rube Who Saved McGraw's Giants*. Los Gatos, CA: Charles April Productions, 2000.

Scheinin, Richard. *Field of Screams: The Dark Underside of America's National Pastime*. New York: W. W. Norton and Co., 1982.

Schneider, Marv. "Those Long-Ago Jewish Boys of Summer." *New York Jewish Week*, June 23, 2009.

Schott, Tom, and Nick Peters. *The Giants Encyclopedia*. Champaign, IL: Sports Publishing, 2003.

Shea, John. "A Giant What-if: Robinson with Mays." *San Francisco Chronicle*, April 15, 2007, C6.

———. "A Giant in His Field, and Now a Hall of Famer." *San Francisco Chronicle*, July 30, 2006, C6.

———. "Giants Honor Former All-Stars." *San Francisco Chronicle*, April 3, 2007, D8.

Stein, Fred, and Nick Peters. *Giants Diary: A Century of Giants Baseball in New York and San Francisco*. Berkeley, CA: North Atlantic Books, 1987.

Thomson, Bobby, with Phil Pepe. *Few and Chosen: Defining Giants Greatness Across the Eras*. Chicago: Triumph Books, 2007.

Tygiel, Jules. "The Polo Grounds." In *American Places: Encounters with History*, edited by William E. Leuchtenberg. Oxford University Press, 2000.

Veeck, Bill, and Ed Linn. "For He's a Jolly Good Fellow." *Sports Illustrated*, May 31, 1965.

Walker, Ben. "Moonlight's 100th: A Century Ago, Graham Got His Only Chance." *New York Daily News*, June 26, 2005.

Weber, Bruce. "Dusty Rhodes, Star Pinch-Hitter in '54 Series, Dies at 82." *New York Times*, June 18, 2009, A25.

Wendel, Tim. *The New Face of Baseball: The One-Hundred-Year Rise and Triumph of Latinos in America's Favorite Sport*. New York: Philip Lief Group, 2003.

Websites

Ballparks.com

Barrypopik.com

Baseball-almanac.com

Baseballanalysts.com

Baseballlibrary.com

Baseballprospectus.com

Baseball-reference.com

bioproj.sabr.org (Baseball Biography Project)

Great-sports-rivalries.com

Historicbaseball.com

Sanfranciscogiants.com

Sfgiants.scout.com

Sportsillustrated.cnn.com

Thebaseballpage.com

Thecolumnists.com

Author Interviews

Roger Angell, telephone interview, January 9, 2008

Larry Baer, in-person interview, AT&T Park, San Francisco, December 17, 2007

Tito Fuentes, in-person interview, AT&T Park, San Francisco, September 20, 2007

Pat Gallagher, telephone interview, November 15, 2007

Duffy Jennings, in-person interview, San Francisco, December 2007

Mike Krukow, telephone interview, January 2008

Bob Leinweaver, telephone interview, April 2007

Bob Lurie, in-person interview, San Francisco, December 12, 2007

Peter Magowan, in-person interview, AT&T Park, San Francisco, November 2007

Willie McCovey, telephone interview, December 2007

J. T. Snow, telephone interview, December 2007

Darryl Spencer, telephone interview, December 5, 2007

Omar Vizquel, in-person interview, AT&T Park, San Francisco, September 2007

Al Worthington, telephone interview, December 11, 2007

Index